I0756445

The Development of State Legislation Concerning the Free Negro

By

FRANKLIN JOHNSON

Submitted in partial fulfilment of the requirements for the Degree of Doctor of Philosophy in the Faculty of Political Science in Columbia University

---

With a new introduction by

Paul Finkelman
President William McKinley Distinguished Professor of Law and Public Policy
Albany Law School

THE LAWBOOK EXCHANGE, LTD.
Clark, New Jersey

ISBN 9781584777519 (hardcover)
ISBN 9781616192747 (paperback)

Lawbook Exchange edition 2007, 2012

The quality of this reprint is equivalent to the quality of the original work.

THE LAWBOOK EXCHANGE, LTD.
33 Terminal Avenue
Clark, New Jersey 07066-1321

Please see our website for a selection of our other publications and fine facsimile reprints of classic works of legal history:
www.lawbookexchange.com

Library of Congress Cataloging-in-Publication Data

Johnson, Franklin, 1875-
The development of state legislation concerning the free Negro / Franklin Johnson; new introduction by Paul Finkelman.
p. cm.
Originally presented as the author's thesis, Columbia University, 1918.
Originally published: New York : Arbor Press, 1918.
Includes bibliographical references.
ISBN-13: 978-1-58477-751-9 (alk. paper)
ISBN-10: 1-58477-751-6 (alk. paper)
1. African Americans--Legal status, laws, etc. 2. Freedmen. I. Title.
KF4757.Z95J63 2007
342.7308'73--dc22 2006018975

Printed in the United States of America on acid-free paper

INTRODUCTION

The Development of State Legislation Concerning the Free Negro is an odd but very important and extremely useful book. Written nearly a century ago, it is an example of the best of the Ph.D. dissertations of the first generation of doctoral students in the social sciences. It lacks any great theoretical framework or much analysis, but it is chock full of information, facts, tables, and excerpts from laws. It is also useful because many of the laws set out in this volume are not easily found otherwise. Despite the massive growth of material on the internet or in machine readable form, early laws are still hard to locate. Anyone interested in the history of segregation and racism will find Johnson's pioneering work invaluable.

Franklin Johnson first wrote this book as a dissertation in political science at Columbia University. Johnson's book was essentially one of basic research on the issue of segregation and race. Published in 1918, at the high tide of segregation, Johnson attempted to offer a comprehensive look at American laws on race. The book was surely timely. Only two decades earlier, in *Plessy v. Ferguson* (1896) the U.S. Supreme Court had given its blessing to segregation, as long as separate public facilities were "equal." That case gave a green light to the southern states – and a few northern states – to pass laws allowing or requiring segregation.

Plessy did not mandate segregation; it only allowed it at the state level. The federal government still supported racial equality and integration. But that too changed starting in 1913 when President Woodrow Wilson entered the White House. A progressive on many issues, the Virginia-born Wilson was more hostile to black equality than any president since Andrew Johnson. Wilson quickly ordered the segregation of federal facilities in Washington. When World War I began his administration arranged for the forced retirement of the highest ranking black officer in the Army, Col. Charles Young so that he would not end up commanding white troops. Although the War was fought to make the world safe for democracy, Wilson insisted on strict segregation in the Army. On the home front lynching was rampant.

In this atmosphere Johnson catalogued and described the legislation in the nation that regulated race relations. Although the book's title indicated it was limited to legislation, Johnson also included discussions of court opinions. Similarly, while the title of the book implies he was only interested in state law, Johnson in fact included a listing of federal laws and U.S. Supreme Court opinions dealing with race.

Some of the information in this book will surprise modern readers, and perhaps even lead scholars to rethink our notions of race relations between the Civil War and World War I. For example, two tables on segregation in education show that from 1871 to 1911 some seventeen states in the North and West repealed laws requiring or allowing segregated schools. This list does not include states like Iowa and Massachusetts, which banned segregated schools before the Civil War, or Vermont, New Hampshire, Oregon, or North and South Dakota, which never had laws requiring segregated schools.

Equally useful, and startling, is Johnson's Chronological Record of Legislation Concerning Civil Rights. In 1883 the Supreme Court overturned the federal Civil Rights Act of 1875, which had mandated equal accommodations in hotels, restaurants, and places of amusement like theaters. This table shows that in response to this decision northern and western states passed more than 40 separate civil rights laws. This table did not include constitutional provisions, such as the one in Wyoming's constitution of 1889 that required that all laws "affecting the political rights and privileges of its citizens shall be without distinction of race, color, sex, or any other circumstance or condition whatsoever other than individual incompetency or unworthiness. . . ."

While the support for civil rights in this period may surprise scholars, the sheer number and level of detail of laws requiring segregation in the South may also astound them. Some of the laws passed to create two societies in the South illustrate the absolute refusal of the South to accept the outcome of the Civil War and the plain meaning of the Amendments that followed the War. Despite the Fourteenth Amendment's requirement of "equal protection" for people of all races, in 1876 Maryland prohibited blacks from becoming lawyers. This remained good law until 1914 when the state opened the bar exam to blacks. Some of the laws seem almost incomprehensible. For example, in 1894 Georgia required that black and white taxpayers be listed separately while 1907 Alabama required that taxes collected from blacks be "kept separate" from taxes collected from whites. Most impressive, perhaps, is the level of detail in the myriad of segregation laws, describing what kinds of signs should indicate facilities for blacks and whites, insuring that convicts of different races not be shackled together, or that schools for the blind separate whites and blacks.

Although nearly a century old, Johnson's book is the starting point for an examination of how states regulated race before World War I. It provides a grim record of much of America's commitment to *inequality* in this period as well as a more positive record of those states that tried to guarantee equality in this period.

Paul Finkelman
President William McKinley Distinguished
Professor of Law and Public Policy
Albany Law School
May 2007

The Development of State Legislation Concerning the Free Negro

By

FRANKLIN JOHNSON

Submitted in partial fulfilment of the requirements for the Degree of Doctor of Philosophy in the Faculty of Political Science in Columbia University

NEW YORK

1918

CONTENTS

PART I

General Development of the Legislation

PART II

A Detailed Review of the Laws

Contents

PREFACE

This monograph deals with the laws, enacted by each of the states of the United States and by the Federal government prior to 1917, which in terms have related specifically to the negro. All laws of this character are included except those relating to slaves and to negroes freed prior to the Civil War, and so-called "private" and "local" laws, and appropriation acts. No attention is paid to laws which in terms do not relate to the negro even though some of the statutes of this character, such as the acts restricting the suffrage and containing a "grandfather" clause, were undoubtedly passed with the purpose of affecting the status of the negro very materially. No attempt has been made to review court decisions. Where, however, laws have been declared void or unconstitutional, such court action has been noted. Various other limitations of the field, for the most part of minor importance, are discussed in the opening chapter. Within this field the aim has been to present a complete record of all enactments, including every amendment no matter how unimportant, and every repeal no matter how small.

The original aim of the author was to review all legislation that had ever in any way affected the negro in this country, in the hope that the material, thus rendered available, might aid in an intelligent understanding of the status of that race. The overwhelming magnitude of the task soon became evident, however, and the scope of the work was limited in the ways already indicated.

It is evident that complete generalizations concerning the general trend of legislation affecting the negro cannot be based on the laws dealt with in this volume alone. Only the carrying out of the original plan would have made possible a valid general summary of the trend of legislation concerning the negro in this country. It is the author's hope, however, that a complete review of the field indicated will prove more valuable than the possible results of an attempt to deal in an incomplete manner with the whole field.

The thorough treatment undertaken has involved much labor and difficult investigation. It would have been impossible except for the libraries of the New York Bar Association and the New York Law Institute, where the larger part of the investigation was done.

Many difficulties arose in the course of the minute and detailed work, which are mentioned more fully later. They include on the one hand difficulties in discovering legislative enactments, and on the other hand difficulties in making sure of the absence of such enactments. Thoroughness and accuracy have been sought and it is hoped have been substantially achieved. Wherever possible each reference has been verified. In a few cases laws have necessarily been accepted as referred to in later statute books, or elsewhere than the original, the latter being no longer available. Many inaccuracies and errors have been found in the statute records themselves.

In addition to the source book value of Part II of this volume it is the hope of the author that the summaries of certain parts of the material, as presented in Part I, will prove useful. These summaries relate mainly to the most important phases of the legislation under review, namely, intermarriage, education, transportation, civil rights and segregation.

This opportunity cannot be passed without a tribute of appreciation to Professor Franklin H. Giddings, who first suggested this line of research and interested the writer in it, and whose high scholarship and broad outlook and vision inspire all who have come into contact with him.

PART I

THE GENERAL DEVELOPMENT OF THE LEGISLATION

CHAPTER I. *The Negro Problem in Legislation*

Among the most fundamental social problems affecting the organization of a society are those which concern its constitution and homogeneity. The presence in the social structure of different portions of the population, with different interests, different functions, and developing along different lines, is a fact of primary significance where it exists. The reactions of one such population group toward another, or of the larger body toward an included group, give rise to phenomena of great importance.

In the United States the negroes form a population group which demands most thoughtful consideration. Their numbers are great and increasing. They have been intertwined vitally into the development and history of the country. Many difficult problems of adjustment have arisen concerning them. Obviously also they cannot in a generation or two be absorbed and disappear as a separate group.

The object of this study is to investigate such phenomena as appear in a special field of the problem of the negro population group. This field in general is the development of legislation concerning the negro in the United States and its commonwealths. Specifically, however, this essay covers but a portion of this general field, as will appear presently when its exact scope is discussed.

Laws may become obsolete or dead letters. Nevertheless, they tend to show the crystallization of public opinion at the time of their enactment, and the method of treatment of a subject by the sentiment of the population as a whole. They also indicate a situation requiring attention, and what is regarded as necessary to meet it. The significance of laws, therefore, is not found only in their complete or continued enforcement. It is also found in their indication of the viewpoint of the governing group in the population and the ideals held by them, which though not always entirely put into practice yet in a measurable degree are effective. Stroud, in his *Sketch of the Laws* says,[1] "In representative republics like the United States where the popular voice so greatly influences all political concerns, and where the members of the legislative departments are dependent for their places upon annual elections, the laws may safely be regarded as constituting a faithful exposition of the sentiments of the people." The laws of a state thus show approximately the preferred method of treatment of a subject, and in large part the actual treatment of the subject. To some extent at least they show at the time of passage, as often as reenacted, and so long as substantially in force, the effective opinion of the community.

The reaction of the public to the negro problem both in the North and in the South has accordingly been manifested in the legislatures of the different states by the adoption of various measures of legislation according to the supposed needs of the time. Legislative provisions parallel the changing situation of the relationship of the white and the colored races, and the development and progress of legislation concerning the negro throws lights on both the history and advancement of that race and on the opinions and viewpoint of the members of the dominant white population. Legislation in regard to the negro with reference to its historical development, therefore, is one of the most important fields of study.

In spite of the great volume of literature which has been published in regard to the negro little has appeared treating of his legal status. Prior to the Civil War, many books of considerable merit on this aspect of the negro question were published. Among these may be mentioned: Goodell, *The American Slave Code* (1853); Wheeler, *A Practical Treatise on the Law of Slavery* (1837); Stroud, *A Sketch of the Laws Relating to Slavery in the Several States* (1858); and Hurd, *The Law of Freedom and Bondage in the United States* (1858 and 1862). The book by Wheeler consists of a compilation of the decisions made on the subjects in the courts, and is a case book or digest. The other books treat of the statute laws regulating the negro race. All of these works, together with others not here named, fully cover the law concerning the negro in slavery or the slave codes. Legislation concerning the free negro is also referred to, and is treated by Hurd in a full and thorough fashion. *The Law of Freedom and Bondage* takes up the subject of legislation concerning the free negro as found

[1] Page v.

in each of the several slave states, and in a number of the free states, this work being an adequate and sufficient authority on such legislation in the slave states up to the time of the Civil War.

Since the Civil War, while there have been numerous brief articles appearing in periodical literature, the field of the legal treatment of negroes in the United States apparently remains untouched with the exception of one book, namely, Stephenson's, *Race Distinctions in American Law.* The object of this book is, in the words of its preface: "The inquiry has been: how much does the negro lack of being, in truth, a full-fledged American citizen? What limitations upon him are allowed or imposed by law because he is a negro?" The book takes up the important lines of legislation, and gives for each subject its various forms and provisions, with the states in which these are the law. It also includes past legislation regarded as important, under each line of legislation, as well as references to court decisions selected from those which comment on and interpret the laws.

The present work has a different field and purpose. It presents a complete record of all legislative enactments, up to 1918, within its scope, which have ever been adopted by any state, and such parts of Federal legislation as will presently be mentioned. The legislation is recorded under the name of each state, and is presented in the chronological order in which it was enacted, the year of each enactment being shown.

The complete record of all acts, chronologically presented, and recorded for each state, shows the subjects and topics of legislation within our field, which it has been considered necessary to adopt in the legislative history of any state. The various times and periods within each state when the legislature took such action are thus presented. The amount of legislation is shown, and the particular lines and kinds, within the field, which have ever been adopted by any state, or which have ever been repealed or modified after previous adoption. Conversely the absence of legislative action on the part of any state is made evident. The progressive development of legislation is presented for each state. The tendencies and the trends are manifested in each state, as they have appeared from time to time. The material is thus made available for the comparative study of the legislation of one state with that of another, or of the legislation of one period with that of another period. Chronological tables of some of the most important lines of legislation are given for convenience of reference.

The general field of the present investigation, as already indicated, is the investigation of the development of legislation concerning the negro. The specific field, however, requires delimitation both chronologically and as to subject matter. Considering the chronological limitation a difference immediately appears between the former slave states and the free states. In the slave states there was, previous to emancipation, a certain amount of legislation concerning the free negro. This as already stated has been thoroughly covered for each state by Hurd. Any further consideration of it would be mere repetition. Moreover, most of it was dissimilar from the lines of present legislation and outside its course of development. This period is therefore not included herein. A second period to consider is that immediately following the Civil War, when in the slave states various laws were passed concerning the freed negro often minutely regulating his position. These laws were only temporary and were both adopted and repealed or omitted from the compiled laws within a brief period, in some cases within a year. Some of them apparently were never put into force. They constitute a single period, without features of inner development important for us, and have been referred to in general literature. Many of them were of great bulk, many pages of detailed regulations appearing in a single act. They were also mostly dissimilar from the lines of present legislation, from which they are separated by the Fourteenth Amendment to the Constitution and by the effect of the Reconstruction administrations in the Southern states. They referred to such subjects as minute regulations of farm labor and duties of the negro, terms of employment, possession of weapons, etc. For these reasons detailed tracing of these laws for each state is not included. For each Southern state therefore the record commences with the first more permanent laws following the Civil War and freedom. The laws of the Reconstruction period are included because although many were later repealed at various dates, they overlap, merge into, and interlink with later legislation in many cases.

For the free states the legislation was not marked by any sharp break such as the Civil War occasioned in the Southern states, but flows in a more nearly continuous stream. It is not possible to select any particular starting place for its development. Therefore for these states the record goes back to the earliest legislative enactments, where necessary antedating statehood, thus including the earliest provincial laws and territorial laws, in spite of the difficulty of ascertaining them.

The delimination of the field of the investigation as to subject matter is indicated by the fact that the essay includes all general legislation mentioning the negro in freedom. Thus all legislation relating to slavery is excluded. The term general legislation excludes so-called private or local laws and money appropriations by the legislature of the state. A few instances of such legislation and of other types of legislation not strictly within the scope of this monograph are included for special reasons. The investigation also excludes court decisions, except where the court holds legislation unconstitutional or otherwise void. A few other court decisions are included for special reasons, noted in each instance.

All legislation, whether in constitution or in session laws, is included which mentions the negro or specifically refers to him, through the use of such words as negro, color, black, white, race, etc., or in any other way, except slave laws, local and private laws, appropriation acts, and such Federal legislation as is indicated in the following paragraphs. Legislation without explicit reference to the negro is not included. There are, of course, certain acts supposed to have been passed with reference to the negro, though containing no mention of him. But to determine whether a given act not mentioning the negro was enacted with special reference to him or not is not always easy and is often a matter of opinion. Among such laws are various vagrancy laws, peonage laws, and the election laws of different Southern states. The least disputed example probably were the so-called "grandfather" clauses of certain Southern election laws, yet even these have been declared otherwise. The limit has perforce been drawn according to the terms of the law and not according to the underlying motives of the legislators. There is also naturally not included each instance of the mere repetition of previously enacted legislation, without alteration, in the course of issuing successive editions of Compiled Statutes, or otherwise repeating general sections of statutes. All alterations, repeals, or even omissions of a law are carefully noted.

Federal legislation differs completely from state legislation, in that it has been thoroughly and carefully indexed, from an early date, the index including past enactments. A long list of all Federal enactments on the subject, major and minor, would be needless duplication, lists of enactments being already accessible in the Federal indexes. Some Federal legislation is included as an aid to understanding the development of state legislation.

Research into existing laws is a less onerous task than an attempt to discover and to record all legislation enacted at any time within a given field. The difficulties in research into the past records of legislation are great. While court decisions are well indexed and contained in numerous digests, there is in most states a total lack of both indexes and digests for past statute law. The current law of a state is contained in the compiled laws or revised statutes of the state, but it is frequently a matter of great difficulty to trace any one of these laws in its development and to its origin. Still harder is it to discover laws which have been long repealed and have therefore disappeared.

In many cases inaccurate indexes were found in the volumes of statutes. Even in volumes of session laws, there are sometimes enactments which have been totally omitted from the index of the volume, and can therefore be discovered only by an actual turning over of all the pages contained in the statute book. This was found to be the case in a number of instances. In many instances a law although indexed is referred to in such a way that no reference whatever to the negro race appears. For example, some of the recent hospital legislation concerning the colored race can be discovered only under the word hospital, the index containing no word whatever indicating its special application to the negro. The indexing of laws is also done under a large number of varying heads, all of which must be examined in every state to cover possible statutes. For example, a separate coach law may be found indexed only under the head of Railroads, in other cases only under Jim Crow, in other cases only under Common Carriers, or again, only under one of the many terms used to indicate the negro, such as Negro, Colored, Black, Race, Mulatto. Search must be made under all of these heads to ascertain the law. If the intent of the index makers had been to conceal the laws contained in the statute books and in the session laws, they could at times have adopted no better plan to accomplish this purpose.

There is also carelessness in the printing of statutes. In a number of cases laws are referred to in later legislation or in court decisions which diligent search failed to reveal in the statute books of the date referred to, or at any other time.

On account of the lack of proper indexing, and in addition the failure of most states to maintain any record of legislation which was later repealed, or as often happened simply omitted, it is even harder to make sure that there was no legislation in a given period than to discover such legislation when it exists. The variation in usage among the different states is great as to their methods of recording or referring to statutes which do not appear in the latest compilation of current laws. An investigation based on court decisions is far easier, for the reasons given, than one into past statutory law.

Legislation mentioning the negro falls naturally into two broad divisions. The first includes enactments in restriction of the negro, or expressing a sentiment opposed to his full and unrestrained intermingling with the activities of the white population. The second includes enactments in protection of the negro, or expressing a sentiment favoring him and his participation in activities. All legislation of both classes is of course here recorded. This division is a natural one for the consideration of the field. The following chapters accordingly consider first restrictive enactments, then protective enactments. Following this, consideration is given to social influences underlying the legislation.

CHAPTER II.

General Development of Restrictive Legislation

For the proper understanding of the course of legislation in the individual states, some knowledge is necessary of the general development of each of the several lines of legislation, as found in the states considered together. Such a view of the legislation is likewise important in itself. This chapter will treat therefore of the outstanding features of the development of legislation in restriction of the negro. Within the scope outlined in the previous chapter it will consider restrictive legislation concerning intermarriage or miscegenation, education, transportation, civil rights, segregation, and miscellaneous provisions. Protective legislation will be considered in the following chapter.

INTERMARRIAGE

Legislation concerning intermarriage or miscegenation is simple in form. In the nature of the case it was not subject to a process of development and growth as to its provisions. It always consisted of the prohibition of intermarriage between any negro and any white person. Two minor modifications are noted later which slightly vary the last term. A penalty for violation of the law was usually imposed. In most states the intermarriage was declared void.

The law against intermarriage made its appearance at an earlier date than any other article of legislation considered, either restrictive or protective.

Most of the states, both Northern and Southern, which enacted such legislation did so prior to the Civil War. Closely following the end of that period, however, four states adopted such an act. After that time no further state, which had not previously done so, adopted an intermarriage prohibition, except Louisiana and except territories which entered late into statehood, namely, Utah, Oklahoma, Montana and South Dakota. Therefore, by far the larger part of all legislation prohibiting intermarriage was first enacted either prior to or just following the Civil War.

The law has been repeated or reenacted with trifling modifications by various states, no special feature marking its course. At no time was there found after 1850 a period of longer than three years without the appearance in some state of such an enactment or reenactment, until 1895.

The law against intermarriage was repealed or omitted by eleven states which at one time had enacted the statute, and in one other state was rendered inoperative through a court decision. The states which repealed or omitted the law, with the date of such action, are Massachusetts, repealed 1840; Iowa, omitted 1851; Maine, omitted 1857, repealed 1883; Kansas, repealed 1859; New Mexico, repealed 1866; Washington, repealed 1867; South Carolina, repealed 1868; Mississippi, omitted 1871; Rhode Island, repealed 1881; Michigan, repealed 1883; Ohio, repealed 1887. The two Southern states of Mississippi and South Carolina later reenacted the law, Mississippi in 1880 by insertion in its Revised Statutes of that date, and South Carolina by reenactment in 1879. In addition to these ten states, the intermarriage law of Alabama was held void by a decision of the state court in 1872, and five years later was again declared valid by a further court decision.

Only three instances of the repeal or omission of the law came before 1865, all the other cases, including its repeal in the state of Maine, dating after the close of the Civil War. None of the instances of permanent repeal or abandonment were in the Southern states.[1] New Mexico is not here classed as a Southern state, and the permanent repeal of the law there was in line with the general legislation of that state, which in its development has opposed discrimination or restriction on account of its large population with Mexican and Spanish blood.

A few states in their earlier statutes formerly imposed a penalty upon the white person but not upon the negro, West Virginia being the only such state at the present time. On the contrary a few imposed a severer penalty upon the negro than upon the white person. A few of the very early statutes also contained extremely severe penalties, such as life slavery, for a free negro violating the law. These early severe penalties have also disappeared. An early provision was also the imposing of a penalty upon the

[1] The term Southern states in this essay has a special meaning, namely, the former slave-holding states.

person performing the ceremony but not upon the parties to the intermarriage. Massachusetts exemplifies this. The theory was, apparently, that the person qualified to perform a marriage ceremony was a person of especial responsibility and intelligence, and since the violation of the law was impossible without his act, the penalty was inflicted solely upon him.

One great object of laws against intermarriage is undoubtedly to prevent race mixture, or as the early act of Massachusetts phrased it, "to prevent spurious and mixed issue." It is a noticeable feature of this legislation that only a few states have ever enacted any laws against illicit intercourse between white and colored persons. Provisions to this effect have been inserted in the law against intermarriage of three states only, Alabama, Florida, and Nevada, while one state only, namely, Louisiana, has provided for it in a separate act.

The two minor modifications in the general provision referring to white persons are as follows: North Carolina in 1871 prohibited also intermarriage of a negro with an Indian, later in 1887 limiting this only to the Croatan Indians, or Indians of Roberson County. Massachusetts in its law referred to in the preceding paragraph forbade negro intermarriage with a person of any Christian nation.

EDUCATION

Restrictive legislation concerning education is directed toward securing separation in education between the negro and the white races. The general form of a separate education law is an act requiring separation in schools and institutions of learning conducted by the state. A second form of the law has been enacted in four Northern states, by which such separation is permitted, but not required, the states being Arizona, Indiana, Kansas, and Wyoming. One other Northern state, namely, New York, while specifically forbidding exclusion from any school on account of color, provides a method of establishing voluntary separate schools. Recent modifications of the above-named general form of the separation law are mentioned later. Legislation prohibiting separation in education will be referred to in another chapter.

Most of the laws thus restricting negro education which were adopted by the Northern states were first enacted either before or very shortly after the close of the Civil War. California first enacted its law in 1869. No other state outside of the group of Southern states enacted for the first time such a law after this, except three states which entered into statehood at a late date, namely, Arizona, Oklahoma, and Wyoming. Restrictive legislation concerning education, outside the Southern states, therefore in general ceased to develop four years after the Civil War, and but for California would have ceased in 1865, subject to the exceptions just named.

Most of the Southern states, contrary to the course of the Northern states, enacted such a law as a definite part of their statutes at varying periods after the Civil War. The reason for this is plain. Previous to that time not only was the public school system in a rudimentary form, but the colored people were slaves. Separation was a matter which in general required no legislation to enforce during the time of slavery. What little legislation was enacted was in total restriction of education for the negro, rather than for separation in education. When slavery ceased, it then became necessary to enact definite requirements of separation to secure it.

No Southern state which ever enacted a separate education law has ever abandoned it, with the temporary exceptions of South Carolina and Louisiana. This is referred to more fully in the following chapter.

In most of the Northern states which restricted education the development of legislation has been away from separation. Separate education laws have been either omitted, or have been replaced by a definite prohibition of separation. The separation requirement has been omitted by Nevada, Ohio, and California as to negroes. Separation has been replaced by definite prohibition in Minnesota, Montana, New York, and Pennsylvania.

The former separate education laws of various states contained requirements which deserve attention. In some states the funds for the support of the negro schools were not drawn from the public school funds in general, but were derived from the taxation of the property of colored persons or from special taxes upon colored people such as poll taxes or special educational taxes. Under these conditions the colored race was charged with the support of its own schools, either wholly or in large part. This provision has disappeared from the law today except in Kentucky where it appears still to be sanctioned. Another feature which formerly appeared in certain states was a provision vesting the control of the negro schools in negro trustees or school boards, instead of placing the separate negro schools under the control of the general school board in each district. This appeared to be a measure of self-government for the negro. It probably operated injuriously to entrust the administration of the schools to people themselves limited in education by necessity, who had few means of acquiring information concerning educational methods. A third feature concerns the minimum number of pupils required in a few states for the maintenance of separate schools, it being provided that when there are fewer children in a district than the required number the school board is not required to maintain separate schools. The tendency has been to reduce the number so required, as seen for example in West Virginia. The states having such requirements at present are Arizona, requiring eight; Maryland, "if the number shall warrant;" Missouri, fifteen; West Virginia, ten; and Wyoming, fifteen.

A noteworthy development of separate education legislation has appeared in certain Southern states, in the late enactment of a requirement compelling separation in all schools and institutions of learning, no matter by whom conducted. The previous laws and the laws of other states require separation in education supported by public funds and administered by the state, that is, in public schools. The new requirement has added private schools. This provision appeared first in Florida in a law of 1895, which was specially designed to include all schools both public and private. Florida had many years before passed a law requiring separation in education, and also had enacted a constitutional requirement to the same effect. In the law of 1895 it extended the previous enactments so that not only public schools and institutions of learning supported by state funds were required to maintain separation of races, but also all educational institutions in the state were under the same requirement. The Florida law forbade conducting either a public or private school where white persons and negroes are instructed in the same building, or in the same class, or at the same time by one teacher. The law imposed a penalty both upon the teacher, and also upon anyone patronizing the school, which included its supporters and its officers.

A law similar in its general provisions to the statute of Florida appeared six years later, in 1901, in Tennessee. It forbade any institution of learning from receiving white and colored pupils together. It also rendered it unlawful for any teacher to instruct them together or to allow it. The penalty was imposed both on any teacher violating the law, and on the institution itself. The laws of Florida and Tennessee resemble each other, and the second was evidently copied in its general terms from the first. They form a class by themselves, distinct from the two later statutes covering the same field, mentioned in the next paragraphs.

A separate education law covering all institutions of learning both public and private was enacted in Kentucky in 1904, three years after the Tennessee act. This was drawn in entirely different terms, and manifested a different spirit from the previous laws just examined. It rendered it unlawful to operate any institute of learning where persons of the two races were received as pupils. It imposed the extremely heavy fine of one thousand dollars together with an added fine of one hundred dollars for each day the institution was operated after conviction. It also imposed the same severe fine upon each individual instructor teaching in any such institution, and this regardless of whether the special instructor had personally taught both races jointly. If the school had one class in which both races were taught together, and the school maintained a staff of twenty instructors, then each instructor would be liable to the fine of one thousand dollars. The act further made attendance at such a school unlawful for each white person and also each negro attending as student, and imposed the heavy fine of fifty dollars for each day any student whatever attended such an institution. The act allowed a separate branch located at least twenty-five miles away for the education of a different race.[2] It will be seen how different this act is from the Tennessee statute. The Kentucky law not only imposed a heavy penalty upon the institution itself and upon any teacher offending, but it also penalized the entire teaching staff of the institution, and the entire student body. The Kentucky statute in question could hardly be more severe unless it made violation a prison offense. The law was directed at the only institution in Kentucky at that time which received both white and negro students, namely, Berea College. This institution was established long before the Civil War for the purpose of the education of the population of the mountain whites in Eastern Kentucky and in the adjoin-

[2] This last provision was held void because unreasonable, by the Kentucky court in 1906.

ing states. Subsequent to the Civil War, negro students were also received, and out of a total number of approximately one thousand students at the time of the enactment of the statute, about one-fifth were colored.

Similar to the Kentucky statute and forming a class with it was the law of Oklahoma of 1908, which apparently copied the Kentucky act, although much more mild in its penalties. The Oklahoma law made it illegal to operate any institution of learning receiving both white and colored students. An offending institution was fined from one hundred to five hundred dollars, and each day it was open was a separate offense. Each teacher of such a school could be fined from ten to fifty dollars a day, and each pupil from five to twenty dollars a day. It will be seen how closely this act was apparently patterned after that of Kentucky, avoiding however the extreme penalties imposed by the latter. It also avoided the provision requiring a separate branch not less than twenty-five miles away for the education of a different race, which had been held void by the Kentucky courts two years before.

These four states are the only ones refusing to allow the same institution to furnish instruction, even though separately conducted, to both the white and colored races, even when such institutions are entirely private in their support, and receive no part of the public state educational funds. The two earlier statutes were mild in tone and carried moderate penalties. The two later statutes were stringent and carried severe penalties.

The most recent development of the separate education legislation of the Southern states is a requirement limiting the instruction of negro children to teachers of the negro race. The majority of the teachers of the negro children are at present of the negro race, and this law prevents instruction except by such, withdrawing the benefit of white instruction. Such a law was enacted by Florida in 1913, being of course reciprocal in its terms.

TRANSPORTATION

Separation in transportation is the most conspicuous form of restriction. The public in general does not often enter schools, and intermarriage between the races is not only rare but not necessarily noticeable when it exists. Separation in public transportation becomes evident at once to any person who travels in the states having such requirements. On this account, it is often the first law which the public thinks of when considering restrictive legislation concerning the negro.

Laws requiring separation in transportation came only after the close of the Civil War. Before the Civil War, while slavery was still in force, such separation was universally compelled, the authority of the white race over the negroes being sufficient for this purpose. Subsequent to the Civil War, the authority of the white race though no longer legally binding was felt as a moral force by the colored race and apparently was sufficient to secure the continuance of such separation in most of the Southern states for a long period after the close of the War, although three such states adopted legislation in somewhat elementary form immediately after the Civil War. A further reason doubtless was the fact that railroad travel was not so prevalent at an earlier period as at present, while the colored population lacked both means and motive for extended and frequent use of railroads. During the Reconstruction period all three states referred to repealed their laws. With the exception of a single state, Tennessee, in 1881, no state enacted a separate coach law or other provision as to separation in transportation until more than twenty years after the Civil War. In 1887, and during the five years following, a number of Southern states adopted this provision, the others following in the years immediately after 1898.

The state which first enacted a definite law requiring separation in public vehicles following the Civil War was Florida, in 1865. The law provided that no negro should intrude himself into any public vehicle set apart for white people. It carried a penalty of standing in the pillory or of being whipped, or both. The law applied equally to any white person intruding into any vehicle for the colored race, under the same penalties. No white person would probably as a matter of fact so intrude, but nevertheless the penalty, especially that of whipping, which was used for the colored race, is noteworthy in its application to the white race, though only in form. In the same year Mississippi enacted a law forbidding the employee of any railroad to permit any negro to ride in cars used for white persons, under penalty of fine and imprisonment. This statute was entirely in restriction of the colored race, and contained no reciprocal clause applying likewise to the white race. Following the example of these two states, Texas enacted a brief provision to the effect that every railroad company was required to attach to each passenger train one car for freed men. This law did not require compulsory separation between the white and negro travellers. It was apparently assumed that the colored freed men would in fact travel in their own car. These three early laws were elementary, and did not reach the well developed form of the later separate coach legislation.

During the Reconstruction period these three laws were repealed. Several Southern states then adopted statutes prohibiting separation in transportation. These will be referred to more fully in the following chapter. They were with one exception afterward repealed.

The next appearance of separation legislation was a provision permitting but not requiring such separation. Such an act was adopted in 1875 by Tennessee and by Delaware, the latter including boats.

The first state to adopt a permanent law requiring separation in railroad trains was Tennessee, which in 1881 adopted a law in many respects similar to the later separate coach laws. It was so worded in the preamble, however, as to indicate that it was intended for the protection of the colored race. The preamble recited that railroad companies had been in the practice of charging the colored passengers first class fare and compelling them to occupy second class cars where smoking was allowed and where there was vulgar or obscene language. The act then required that railroad companies should furnish separate cars or separate apartments, for all colored passengers paying the first class rate of fare. These apartments were to be equal in all respects to the first class cars, and were to be subject to their rules in regard to smoking and obscene language. It will be noticed that the penalty consisted of a fine of three hundred dollars to go to the common school fund, which could be recovered by suit of the superintendent of public instruction of the county concerned.

The example of Tennessee was followed six years later by Florida, which was the original state to enact a separate coach law, the Tennessee act apparently being in the minds of the legislators. The law was drawn in terms which provided for the protection of the negro race. It required railroad companies to sell first class tickets to negroes at the same rate as to white persons and to give them equal accommodations. No white person was allowed to ride in a car for negroes or to insult or annoy any negro in the car. No negro was allowed in any car for whites. This law was not yet in the fully developed form which appeared at a somewhat later period, and it had not eliminated the statement of a desire to protect the colored race as well as to enforce its separation. The following year the state of Mississippi again followed the example of Florida, and enacted a separate coach law. This law did not follow the act of Florida in reciting provisions for the protection of the colored race and is much more closely in the form of later legislation, though not so fully developed. It is notable because it is the first law having any provision as to separation of the races in railway stations. This was not required, but the railroad commission was authorized to provide separate rooms, in their discretion. A year later, in 1889, Texas, which was the third state to pass a separate coach law in the previous period, again occupied the same position in this group, and enacted a statute which was passed by the legislature under suspended rule on account of the need of haste.

In the period from 1887 to 1894, in addition to the states already named, separate coach laws were also enacted by Louisiana, Alabama, Arkansas, Georgia and Kentucky. These laws require no special comment except that Louisiana and Arkansas both required separation in railway stations, and Georgia included in its law electric and street cars, in which separation of passengers in the seats was required as far as practicable. This was the first appearance of the later laws requiring separation on electric and street railways.

After 1894 there was a period of four years during which no legislation was enacted. In 1898 the subject again received attention, and the remaining Southern states, with the exception of Delaware and Missouri, adopted laws similar to those of the earlier states, except that in most cases they were in fuller and more developed form. Many of the states also strengthened their previous legislation. This period was also marked by the extension of the requirement of separation on electric and street railways.

While the provisions of the laws requiring separation of the races by railroads differ somewhat in detail, yet in their general terms they are alike. They require separation by means of either entirely separate cars for each race, or by means of a partition dividing a car into compartments, one for each race. In almost every case the railroad is allowed to use either one of these methods. It will be noted that the state of South Carolina, however, requires separate cars only, in its law of 1900, and Maryland requires separate cars only in certain counties, by law of 1908. The partition is required to be substantial, the law often stating that it must be made of wood. Most of the states also have the requirement that the separate compartment must be labelled or marked with a sign indicating for which race it is intended. The laws all provide that the accommodations for each race must be equal, and that there must be no discrimination therein between races.

Street railway transportation developed generally later than railroads, and the legislation referring to it would be expected at a later period than railroad legislation. The first statute containing this requirement, however, was that of Georgia in 1891, which remained isolated until 1901 and 1902, when statutes of limited application appeared in Virginia. By a limited law is meant one not applying to all the street railways of the state, the laws of Tennessee and South Carolina being also of this class. The next statute requiring general separation upon street railways was adopted by Louisiana in 1902, and provided that all street railways must furnish separate but equal accommodations. This was followed in rapid succession, in the order named, by Arkansas, a limited law in Tennessee, Mississippi, Florida, South Carolina, a general law in Tennessee, a general law in Virginia, Texas, Oklahoma, and Maryland.

The provisions of these statutes usually require that the street railway shall maintain either two cars or else one car divided by a partition, which is not generally required to be of wood but which may consist of a wire screen, while in some cases a mere sign placed at the dividing point is sufficient. In a few cases simple separation in the seats of the car is required.

Sleeping and chair cars have been included in the separation requirement of some states. Texas and Oklahoma have required complete separation in all such cars, and Georgia has added the further provision that nothing in the act shall compel sleeping car companies to carry persons of color in their cars. The last statute to this effect was that of Texas in 1914, which provided that the porter of no sleeping car shall be allowed to sleep in any empty berth which is intended for the use of white persons, and also forbids him to use the same bedding as is kept for the use of white persons.

In addition to separation in railroad coaches and cars of electric and street railways, there are also certain other forms of separation connected with transportation. Six states have required separation in railroad stations, either in the waiting rooms, or in the waiting rooms and other facilities of the station. The first state which enacted such a requirement, as already seen, was Mississippi, which in 1888 authorized such separation. The separation was afterward made compulsory. The next state to enact similar legislation was Arkansas in 1893. Following this came Virginia, in a law which allowed the establishment of separate waiting rooms in all stations, and compelled separate waiting rooms at wharves with certain exceptions, and next Florida, Oklahoma, and Texas. South Carolina has not required separation in the waiting rooms of railroad stations by its law, but in 1906 enacted a statute requiring separation in restaurants and eating houses of railroad stations. Separation is in fact provided, although without legislative requirement, in the different Southern states.

Separation upon boats and steamboats has also been required by four states, Maryland, Virginia, North Carolina, and South Carolina. These states all have more or less water traffic, for which reason such a law was natural as a supplement to the separate coach laws of these states. The South Carolina law provided that "all steam ferries" should have separate accommodations. This apparently covered the boats carrying passengers within state waters, and was in effect the same as the laws of the other states named. In addition to these states, Delaware in 1875 allowed separation on boats, though not requiring it. These states are all contiguous and occupy what may be called the northern portion of the southern section of the Atlantic seaboard. Other Southern states, although having considerable water transportation, which have not enacted any such provision, are Florida, Louisiana, Mississippi, and Texas.

CIVIL RIGHTS

Legislation restricting or tending to restrict the negro in regard to certain of his civil rights has been enacted in four Southern states. Such a provision may be termed an Anti-Civil-Rights law. All of this legislation was enacted between 1866 and 1876, inclusive.

The first statute of this nature appeared in the Florida act of 1866 which in addition to prohibiting colored people from intruding into a railroad car for whites also prohibited them from intruding themselves into any public assembly of white persons. This provision while in the nature of an Anti-Civil-Rights law is very brief compared to other and later enactments. Delaware passed a resolution in 1873 declaring opposition to the proposed Act of Congress known as the Supplemental Civil Rights Bill and all other measures intended to equalize the negro race with the white race. It also proclaimed unceasing opposition to the admission of negroes on terms of equality with white people to public conveyances, places of amusement and other places. Two years later Delaware passed another statute to the effect that no keeper of any place of public entertainment or refreshment, no proprietor of any public place or amusement, and no common carrier, were required to admit any person whose presence would be offensive to the major part of the patrons of the place. It has never been repealed and still appears upon the statute books of Delaware although in effect probably a dead letter. In the same year Tennessee passed an Anti-Civil-Rights law still more comprehensive in terms. It abrogated the rule of common law giving a right of action to any person excluded from any hotel, public means of transportation, or place of amusement. It provided that no keeper of any hotel, common carrier, or keeper of a place of amusement, should be under any obligation to admit any person whom he should for any reason whatever choose not to admit, and that the keepers of such places, including common carriers, should have the same right to control admission as that of any person over his private house. This statute was intended to avoid the effect of the Federal Civil Rights law of 1875. It attempted to do this not by creating any distinction between the white and colored race, but by making places formerly public into private places as far as the control of their managers is concerned. This applied to all people alike, and separation was secured by the action of the manager of each place. While this law has never been formally repealed, it has been in part superseded by the separate coach legislation of the state, and in part has become a dead letter.

One more law in the nature of an Anti-Civil-Rights statute requires mention. It is a resolution of the legislature of North Carolina, passed in 1876. It made no change in the operation of the law of the state. It simply declared the repugnance of the General

Assembly of the state to the "Absurd attempts, by means of Civil Rights Bills, to eradicate certain race distinctions."

SEGREGATION

By the term segregation is meant the restriction or limiting of certain portions or districts of a city or community in their use by both races jointly. In one sense all separation is segregation, but the term has come to be employed generally with the significance given above, and it is therefore so used here. The statutes apply equally to negroes and white persons, for otherwise they would be invalid. There have been various local ordinances concerning segregation, in different communities.

The first appearance of such legislation enacted by any state was the Separate Park Law of Georgia, adopted in 1905. This was permissive only, and not compulsory. It provided that any park which was granted to a Municipal Corporation by the owner of the land might in the conveyance be limited to the use of one race only, thus excluding members of the other race. It also provided that a Municipal Corporation might accept the land as a park for the exclusive use of the class named. It need not be said that the holders of city real estate suitable for parks were in most cases white persons, and that the act was likely to be applied with reference to the inclusion of the white population and the exclusion of the colored.

The principle of segregation appeared in more developed form in Louisiana in 1912, in an act which authorized Municipal Corporations to withold building permits for erecting houses for negroes in a white community, or any portion of a community inhabited principally by white people. The same provision was also made throughout as to colored communities. Such a house could only be built with the written consent of the majority of those of the opposite race in the portion to be affected. A "white community" or a "negro community" was defined to mean any subdivision or portion of a town, or any street, inhabited principally by members of the one race. In case of violation of the law, not only was a heavy fine imposed, but the municipality was given the right to remove and to destroy the building.

In the same year Virginia enacted a law of the same general kind but still more expanded, to prevent not only erection of buildings for negroes in the white district, and the reverse, but also to prohibit the residence of any negro in a white district, and the reverse. The law recited that public morals and order would be endangered by the residence of white and colored people in close proximity to each other, and directed that in any town adopting the act, the entire area should be divided into districts known as "Segregation Districts." It required the preparation of a map showing all such districts, and showing the number of white and colored persons in each segregation district. Every district containing more residents of the white race was to be designated as a white district, and a district containing as many, or more, residents of the colored race was to be designated as a colored district. It was rendered unlawful for any negro not already residing in a white district to move into it, either to occupy a house or as a lodger or boarder, the only exception being in the case of servants or members of families living in the district. The same provision was made as to negro districts.

MISCELLANEOUS RESTRICTIVE PROVISIONS

In addition to the subjects which have already been considered, concerning which restrictive legislation has been enacted, there are also other forms of restrictive enactments affecting the negro. Many of these provisions have disappeared from the law. Others were adopted by a single state or a limited number of states, or were otherwise of minor importance. This section will take up in the following order restrictions upon the negro concerning testimony, practising law, jury service, suffrage, state troops, homesteads, custody of white children, exciting race prejudice, saloons, care of sick, state institutions. Various other minor provisions have been included in the terms of several enactments, which are not of sufficient importance to justify detailed mention in this summary.

The testimony of negroes, in legal proceedings, was formerly restricted in a number of states. Prior to the Civil War several of the Northern states adopted provisions in their statutes which forbade the testimony of a negro in any action concerning a white person. The laws varied in the different states, but in substance they were similar, and require no detailed analysis. The states were Indiana, Nebraska, Nevada, Ohio, and Oregon. At or immediately following the close of the Civil War, a few Northern states and a number of Southern states adopted acts restricting the testimony of negroes in general to cases in which white men were not concerned, or else in which white persons were not parties. These states were Alabama, Arkansas, Florida, Georgia, Indiana, Kentucky, Maryland, Nevada, Mississippi, Tennessee, Texas, Washington, and Virginia.

None of these statutes were enacted after 1866, doubtless on account of the Federal Civil Rights Act of that year, which specifically included the right to give evidence. All such statutes have been repealed either by definite enactment or by omission, and in no state is there any restriction upon negro testimony, all restrictive provisions referring now merely to general credibility, intelligence, and similar subjects.

The right of the negro to practice law as an attorney and member of the bar was prohibited by statutory enactment in two states. In Iowa only white males were permitted to practice until 1870. In Maryland admission to the bar was limited to the white race until 1904, when the restriction was omitted. In 1914 the state adopted a provision opening admission to the bar to all qualified persons. No restriction upon this right appears in any state at the present time.

The right of a negro to serve as a juror was restricted after the Civil War by Arkansas, Mississippi and Tennessee. The other Southern states refused in fact to receive negroes upon juries generally. The Federal Civil Rights Act of 1875 contained a special clause, which is still in force, prohibiting disqualifying persons from jury service on account of color. All laws to the contrary in these states therefore became void.

The right of the negro to the ballot was withheld before the year 1870 by the Southern states and many of the Northern states. The only Northern states allowing the ballot to the negro before 1865 were the New England states of Maine, New Hampshire, Vermont, Massachusetts, Rhode Island; and New York and Wisconsin. The latter state extended suffrage to the negro in an act of 1849 which provided for a popular election on the question. The majority of the votes was in favor of negro suffrage, but through a misconception of the law it was declared defeated. In 1866 the courts of the state held that the right had actually been conferred in 1849, and it must therefore be recognized as of that date, although not actually enjoyed by the colored population until the later date. New York state allowed negro suffrage but provided higher qualifications for negroes than for white citizens. With these exceptions no state appears to have extended the right of suffrage to the negro until the close of the Civil War.

Between 1865 and 1870, the date of the Fifteenth Amendment, four more states and territories, all neighboring to Wisconsin, granted to the colored race the right to vote. They were Iowa, Minnesota, and North Dakota and South Dakota, then not separated. The Reconstruction constitutions of the Secession states provided the same.

The whole question of the restriction of suffrage for the colored race was definitely settled by the Fifteenth Amendment in 1870. This provided that the right of any citizen of the United States to vote should not be denied or abridged by any state on account of color. The Fourteenth Amendment had already provided for the citizenship of the negro. Subsequent to the Fifteenth Amendment, therefore, no law was valid which limited the right of the negro to vote, and automatically all the existing laws were made void, whether statutes or constitutional provisions. Since 1870 there have been no restrictions of suffrage by any laws mentioning the negro, or applying in terms to him. Various states have certain provisions in their election laws which apply alike to both races, but which in operation may, in fact, bear more heavily upon the negro, such as the so-called "grandfather clauses," previously referred to, but consideration of these is without our scope.

The service of negroes in state troops or militia has been restricted in four Southern states. Such service was prohibited or abolished by South Carolina in 1865, Arkansas in 1867 (in a statute of somewhat doubtful application), and Georgia in 1905. North Carolina in 1868 merely provided for separation of negro and white members of the militia.

Restrictions as to homesteads, custody of white children, and exciting race prejudice, are as follows. Kentucky in its Homestead Act of 1865, specially provided that the benefits of the act should not apply to the colored race. The act has since been repealed. A law providing that no white child should be permanently placed in the custody of any member of the colored race was enacted in South Carolina in 1910. The act did not apply to the care of a white child by servants or members of the household, but to the permanent care of a white child by such persons, or by any other members of the negro race. The law is still in force. Exciting race prejudice or antagonism is the general field of the acts of two states. Virginia in 1877 prohibited conspiracy to incite the colored population to insurrection, or similarly the white population, the act still being retained upon the current statute book. Kentucky in 1906 rendered it unlawful to participate in any play based upon antagonism alleged formerly to exist between master and slave, or which would excite race prejudice.

Separation in saloons was required in Louisiana in 1908, in an act making it unlawful for any place serving intoxicating beverages to permit their sale for consumption on the premises to whites and negroes within the same building. It will be noticed that this refers not to the same bar-room but to the same building.

A new tendency has appeared regarding separation in the care of the sick, in two of the Southern states. North Carolina in 1915 adopted an act requiring that every institution for the care of the sick in the state, both public and private, should provide colored nurses to care for the colored patients, a fine being imposed in case of violation upon the organization or individual offending. In the same year Alabama adopted a much more stringent law, which rendered it unlawful for any white female nurse to nurse in wards or rooms in any hospital in the state, whether public or private, in which negro men are placed. This rendered it unlawful not only for a white nurse to care for a colored man, but also for a white nurse to care for a white person in a room containing a negro man. The penalty is heavier than that of the North Carolina act, including possible imprisonment in addition to fine. These two laws are significant as introducing a line of separation which has not before been required by legal enactment.

Separation of negroes and white persons in state institutions such as prisons, reformatories, and homes for the blind and other defectives, has been maintained in the Southern states since any such activity was instituted, in general. Separation in prisons, reformatories, or other institutions, has been either recognized or required in the laws of Alabama, Arkansas, Florida, Georgia, Maryland, Mississippi, North Carolina, and South Carolina. Separation in asylums for the insane is either recognized or required in the laws of Georgia, Kentucky, Louisiana, Maryland, Mississippi, Tennessee, and West Virginia. No other state contains any such legal requirement.

CHAPTER III

General Development of Protective Legislation

This chapter will treat of the outstanding features of the development of the several lines of protective legislation, in the states taken together. The most important legislation of this nature is civil rights legislation. It is the most common form of state protective legislation, and often includes various provisions in a single act. After considering civil rights legislation, other protective enactments will be taken up, concerning education, transportation, life insurance regulation, jury service, and miscellaneous provisions. Some of these subjects are included within certain civil rights laws.

CIVIL RIGHTS

The term "civil rights" refers to the rights possessed by an individual under the civil law, and the civil rights legislation of the different states affecting negroes is directed to securing the rights of the colored race under the civil law.

This legislation has been of two distinct kinds, one referring to such rights in general, and the second referring to a special portion of the field. The first class of legislation is that protecting the negro in his general rights under the civil law; such as his right equally with white citizens to make contracts, to hold and convey both real and personal property, to the free use of the courts, and in general to all measures directed toward the security of either person or property. The second class of legislation is that directed specially toward that portion of the field which consists of the right of the negro to the accommodations of places of public resort, with sometimes other specific additions. In order to understand the development of such legislation in the United States it will be necessary to review briefly the Federal enactments upon the subject. Both classes of legislation have been passed by Congress, but only the second class has in general been passed by the different state legislatures.

In considering Federal enactments concerning the first class of legislation, just referred to, it is necessary first to speak of the

Thirteenth Amendment. This provided that neither slavery nor involuntary servitude should exist in the United States. At first sight this may not seem to refer to rights before the civil law. How far it extends over this field has been the subject of many court decisions, holding that the scope of this amendment was wider than merely prohibiting physical slavery as an institution, and that it also affected civil freedom. This point will be found developed more fully by referring to the Civil Rights Cases of 1883, and examining the majority and minority opinions.

In actual practice the precise scope of the civil rights effect of this Amendment has not proved of great importance, in part because it was soon followed by the Civil Rights Act of 1866. This act established the citizenship of all negroes, and then provided specially that regardless of race and color all citizens should be entitled to the same rights under the civil law, especially reciting the right of making contracts, of equality in the courts, of inheriting, receiving, holding and conveying property of all kinds, and in general to the full and equal benefit of all laws and proceedings enjoyed by white citizens. This act belonged to the first-named class of the laws concerning civil rights. It covered the whole field by broad enactment. It also provided a penalty consisting of either fine or imprisonment, or both. This statute was passed by Congress over the veto of President Johnson.

The subject of protection of the colored race in their rights before the civil law was of such importance that Congress felt it should rest upon a firmer foundation than an Act of Congress. It was also desirable to remove all question of the constitutionality and validity of the law of 1866. In view of the Dred Scott decision it was also necessary to provide for the citizenship of the negro race in a positive and certain manner. For these reasons, Congress adopted, in the same year, the Fourteenth Amendment, which was ratified and proclaimed two years later. This amendment was practically identical with the law of 1866, framed in terms suitable for the Constitution. It provided for the citizenship of all persons either born or naturalized in the United States. It next recited that no state should either make any law or enforce any existing law in abridgement of the privileges or immunities of citizens, nor deny to any person the equal protection of the laws. The Fourteenth Amendment did not refer specifically to either race, color, or previous condition of servitude, but was specially directed toward protection of the negro, as has been held by the courts many times, the leading case upon the point being the so-called Slaughter-House Cases of 1872, where the court pronounced that the recent Amendments, the Thirteenth, Fourteenth and Fifteenth, were all specially directed toward the freedom of the slave race and the protection of the newly made free men. The Fourteenth Amendment, following the previous law of 1866, established the general rights of the colored race before the civil law. Many decisions in interpretation of it have been rendered, which have both applied the provisions of the amendment to many specific points and have also refused to apply them. For example, it has been held that the exclusion of negroes from juries on account of color is an abridgement of the Fourteenth Amendment. On the other hand it has been held that separate schools for children of different races do not violate it.

Legislation of this first class, as above referred to, appeared in none of the statutes of the separate states, except Connecticut. The reason for this was the sufficiency of these statutory and constitutional provisions. It has not been necessary either before this date or subsequent to it for any state to pass a measure of general application.

When we examine the second class of legislation, or that providing for protection of the colored race in enjoyment of the accommodations of places of public resort, the case is quite different. The first act of this kind appeared in Massachusetts in a statute of 1865. This provided simply that no distinction or discrimination on account of race should be lawful in any licensed inn, public place of amusement, public conveyance, or public meeting. This was previous to the Civil Rights Act of 1866 of Congress. It was followed in 1866 by a statute very similar in terms, making it unlawful to exclude persons from or restrict them in any licensed public place of amusement, public conveyance, public meeting, or licensed inn, except for good cause. This omitted the reference to race or color and made the law general in its application, safeguarding it by the clause "except for good cause." It will be noticed that these two Civil Rights laws of Massachusetts both apply to public conveyances, and in this respect antedate the law upon that subject enacted in 1867 by Pennsylvania.

During the Reconstruction period of the Southern states, a number of such states enacted Civil Rights laws, which were very full and stringent in their terms. South Carolina was the first state so to provide, being followed by Louisiana, Texas, Arkansas, Florida and Mississippi. Missouri indeed antedated even South Carolina by a brief and ineffectual clause in its constitution of 1865, but it enacted no subsequent legislation. The longest and most stringent of these acts was that of Arkansas. All of these Southern Civil Rights statutes were repealed either by special enactment to that effect or by omission from the Revised Statutes of their states after the end of the Reconstruction period, except such as were found not to be inconsistent with the trend of later legislation, through later interpretation of their precise terms.

There was no further legislation in the Northern states upon this subject until 1873, when New York adopted a Civil Rights Act somewhat similar to that of Massachusetts, but in a fuller and more developed form. The next provision was in New York again, in 1881, which substantially reenacted the earlier provision, and prohibited discrimination in the enjoyment of the accommodations of taverns, public conveyances, and places of public resort or amusement, because of race, creed or color.

Between these two laws, however, came the Federal Act of 1875, known as the Civil Rights Act of that year. This followed in general terms the provisions of the Massachusetts and the New York statutes. It contained a preamble which was copied by the laws of several states. It then provided that all persons should be entitled to full and equal enjoyment of the accommodations and privileges of inns, public conveyances on land and water, theatres, and other places of public amusement, subject only to conditions applicable alike to citizens of every race. The penalty for violation of this law was both a forfeiture to the person aggrieved and fine or imprisonment for the violator. In addition to these general provisions the Civil Rights Act of 1875 also contained a clause specially prohibiting discrimination in jury service.

This law did not accomplish its purpose, for after its passage negroes still continued to be excluded from places of public resort. This resulted in a number of cases appearing in the courts, finally culminating in the so-called Civil Rights Cases, which were passed upon by the United States Supreme Court in 1883. These cases arose in Missouri and Tennessee in the South, and New York, Kansas and California in the North, and were brought for denying to negroes the accommodations of hotels, theatres and railroads. The New York case was for discrimination in the Grand Opera House. By a divided vote the Supreme Court held that the law of 1875, insofar as it applied to the right of accommodation of the colored race in places of public resort, was unconstitutional and therefore void. The provision as to discrimination in jury service was held constitutional.

This decision rendered it impossible for Congress to pass any general enactment prohibiting the passage of laws by individual states concerning the separation of negroes in places of public resort. No further legislation of this nature therefore appeared among the Federal statutes. All further legislation in this portion of the field was thereby thrown into the jurisdiction of the separate states.

This did not greatly affect legislation appearing in the Southern states, for the reason that separation in places of public resort in most cases already existed and was enforced by the power of custom and the influence of the white race. It was followed, however, by enactments requiring separation in railroad transportation. These statutes had appeared before, but their general adoption came after this date, the Federal law of 1875 having included public conveyances on land or water.

The effect in the Northern states was quite different. These states, finding that the negro was no longer protected in this portion of the field of his civil rights by Federal legislation, proceeded to enact separate state laws covering the same ground in general. The year following the Supreme Court decision, four states passed such statutes, being followed successively by a large number of others. Civil Rights laws have been enacted by the following states; California, Colorado, Connecticut, Illinois, Indiana, Iowa, Kansas, Massachusetts, Michigan, Minnesota, Nebraska, New Jersey, New York, Ohio, Pennsylvania, Rhode Island, Washington and Wisconsin.

The Civil Rights laws of the different states usually contained certain general provisions, and also certain specific references under one or more of these provisions. The general provisions of the different laws are very similar. The specific provisions vary considerably in the different states.

In regard to the general provisions, the laws provide that all persons shall be entitled to the full and equal accommodations of inns, public conveyances on land and water, and places of public accommodation or amusement. They make exception of conditions and limitations established by law and applicable alike to all citizens, without regard to race, color or previous condition of servitude. They all carry a penalty for violation, consisting usually of either fine or imprisonment. Many of the laws provide a forfeit to the person aggrieved. In some cases the payment of such a forfeit is a bar to criminal prosecution, and the reverse. There is no exception whatever in any state as regards the insertion of the clause concerning places of public amusement. Every state except California has the provision concerning public conveyances. The provision as to inns appears also in the laws of every state having any Civil Rights enactment, with the exception of Connecticut. The early Civil Rights act of Connecticut was drawn in different terms from those of the other states, it being modelled somewhat after the terms of the Fourteenth Amendment. In 1905 Connecticut passed a law resembling those of other states, but containing only clauses of general application. Inns would no doubt be regarded as included under its clause "Any place of public accommodation."

In regard to the specific references, the laws of every state with the exception of Connecticut, whose law as just said contained only general provisions, and New Jersey and Rhode Island, all forbade distinction in eating houses by appropriate words. One or more of such terms are used as restaurants, chop houses, eating houses, lunch counters, boarding houses, etc. This point may be covered in both New Jersey and Rhode Island by the word inns. All of the states except Connecticut, Kansas, Rhode Island and Wisconsin, also specifically mentioned theatres, following the Federal Civil Rights Act of 1875 in this respect. Special mention of theatres seems unnecessary, as they are undoubtedly included in places of public amusement, which were covered by every law. It is interesting to note that the laws of all the states except five, namely Connecticut, Kansas, New Jersey, Pennsylvania, and Rhode Island, also specifically included barber shops. Court decisions have held in several states that these were not included under the term places of public accommodation, and herein is probably the reason for the general inclusion of them in the laws. Various other specific places were included occasionally, such as music halls, skating rinks, ice cream parlors and soda fountains, elevators, public meetings, etc. These were simply amplifications of the general provisions of the law, inserted to meet local necessities. Saloons were included in the laws of Minnesota and Wisconsin and no distinction is allowed therein in those states. Colorado at one time prohibited discrimination in churches, but this provision disappeared in a later statute.

EDUCATION

Legislation forbidding separation in schools or in education was adopted almost exclusively after the Civil War. Only one state adopted a clear provision to that effect before that time, namely Massachusetts, while Iowa adopted legislation somewhat doubtful in effect. Massachusetts in 1855 enacted a statute which prohibited distinction or exclusion from any public school on account of race, color, or religious opinion. The right to recover damages was given for any child so excluded. Iowa in its constitution of 1857 directed the education of "all the youths of the state." A restrictive statute was adopted soon after, which was held void on the ground that the terms of the constitution rendered it unlawful to exclude colored children from public schools or to compel them to attend separate schools.

In the Reconstruction period two Southern states in 1868 adopted in their constitutions provisions forbidding separate institutions of learning. South Carolina provided that all public schools and institutions of learning supported in whole or in part by the public funds should be open to all students without regard to race or color. Louisiana provided that no separate institution of learning should be established exclusively for any race. Both of these provisions were afterward omitted from the law without formal repealing.

It was more than fifteen years after Massachusetts adopted its law before any further state than those named followed its example. In 1871 Michigan enacted a requirement somewhat similar in effect. In 1873 New York and in 1874 Kansas adopted in their civil rights laws a prohibition of discrimination in public schools. Kansas, however, later allowed separation, as mentioned elsewhere. From time to time different states later adopted similar provisions, none of them being Southern states. The states having laws prohibiting exclusion or discrimination in public schools are Colorado, Idaho, Illinois, Iowa, Massachusetts, Michigan, Minnesota, Montana, New Jersey, New Mexico, New York, Pennsylvania, Rhode Island, and Utah.

Separation in education was previously either permitted or required in three of these states, New York, Montana, and Pennsylvania, which have thus reversed completely their earlier policy. Nevada, Ohio, and California have simply omitted former separation requirements.

Absolute prohibition of any compulsory separation in schools is not inconsistent with voluntary separation on the part of the negro himself. An example of this is found in New York, whose law specifically provides that no person shall be refused admission into or be excluded from any public school on account of race or color. Side by side, with this the law also provides a method of establishment of separate schools for the instruction of colored children in a school district. Where such a school is established, as is the case in New York City, the negro children are under no legal compulsion to attend it. Such separate schools therefore exist in New York from no compulsion in the law, but through the consent of the colored children themselves and their parents and guardians.

Only one Northern state having adopted a prohibition of separation in education has ever repealed the law, namely, Arizona, which in 1909 took such action after only eight years experience with the act, and now permits separation. Kansas, which formerly forbade separation, without repealing its previous law now allows separation in limited form. Wyoming had no legislation in regard to this until 1887, when it adopted a law requiring separation.

TRANSPORTATION

Provisions protecting the negro in his use of public conveyances and prohibiting discrimination have been enacted in a number of states. The first appearance of such legislation was in 1865, when Massachusetts in its Civil Rights law of that year included public conveyances, thereby prohibiting restriction in them on account of color. A general provision of the constitution of 1857 of Iowa was later construed by the state courts as prohibiting separation in transportation, but this cannot be called a law concerning transportation. Following the brief provision of Massachusetts, the next enactment appeared in 1861 in Pennsylvania, which state, influenced possibly by the separation legislation just adopted by three Southern states, enacted a requirement to the opposite effect. It prohibited any railroad from excluding any person from its cars on account of race or color, or from attempting to compel any person to occupy any particular part of a car for the same reason, and imposed a forfeit of five hundred dollars to be paid to the person aggrieved, in addition to a penalty upon the railroad agent committing the offence.

A number of the Southern states, possibly following the example of Pennsylvania, within the next five years enacted laws prohibiting discrimination in public conveyances. Louisiana in its Civil Rights law of 1869 inserted an extended provision with the somewhat curious wording that common carriers should have the right to refuse to admit any person to their cars or other vehicles, when guilty of disorderly conduct or of a breach of the regulations of the company, providing that the regulations made no discrimination on account of race or color. This law was probably intended as a prohibition of separation in public transportation. It will be seen by an examination of its wording that it did not in fact establish this, and accordingly the law has never been repealed but still remains in the statute books of the state. In the same year Mississippi adopted in its Reconstruction constitution a clause forbidding the infringing of the rights of all citizens to travel upon all public conveyances. During the following years of the Reconstruction period Georgia also prohibited separation in transportation, and the early separation laws of Florida and Texas were likewise replaced by specific provisions against separation. Arkansas also adopted a provision against such separation. All of these laws later disappeared, except that of Mississippi.

The further development of the prohibition of separation in transportation came through the Civil Rights laws of the various states. No further state adopted a separate provision to such effect, except as above stated. Every state which has a Civil Rights law, with the single exception of California, has included in it public vehicles or equivalent words, thereby prohibiting restriction or discrimination therein.

MISCELLANEOUS PROTECTIVE PROVISIONS

In addition to the protective legislation already considered, various other protective provisions are of sufficient importance to justify mention, including enactments concerning life insurance, state troops, jury service, testimony, practising law, suffrage, administration of charity, and minor provisions.

Protective legislation prohibiting discrimination or restriction by life insurance companies in the issuance of policies was adopted in several states. Massachusetts, which was the first state to enact a Civil Rights law, was also in 1884 the first state to enact the prohibition of this form of discrimination. This was followed in turn by statutes of Connecticut, Ohio, New York, and Michigan, the last named in 1893, since which time no further legislation of this kind has been adopted. The laws of these states were very similar. They prohibited any life insurance company from making any distinction between white and colored persons in premium or rates, and forbade the company to add any stipulation by which a sum less than the face value of the policy might be paid upon it. In some cases if any colored person was refused, the company when requested was required to issue to him a certificate of the examining physician certifying that the refusal was not on account of the race of the applicant. These provisions were not incorporated into the Civil Rights laws of the respective states, but enacted in separate form.

Negroes have been specially recognized in the state troops or militia in several states. Connecticut in 1879 authorized the organization of four companies of infantry to be composed of colored men. These companies were to be independent and not attached to any existing regiment, unless in case of actual military service. This was a recognition of colored companies already existing in Connecticut. In 1883 reenacting and modifying its law as to militia, the state repealed the militia law of 1879, but specially provided that this should not affect the organization of the colored companies of infantry. New York state at the early date of 1814 authorized the governor to raise two regiments of free men of color, for the defence of the state. The regiments were to be formed into a brigade. All commissioned officers of the company were directed to be white men. Almost one hundred years later in 1913 New York again provided for an additional colored regiment of infantry in the City of New York, which was to be a part of the National Guard of the state, subject in all respects to their regulations. No provision as to the officers of this regiment being either white or colored appeared. New Jersey in 1895 provided that there should be organized four companies of colored infantry in that state, which were to be separate companies, but incorporated in the regular militia. Michigan in 1901 provided that if more than forty companies of infantry were organized, at least one must be composed of colored men. In the law of 1905 referring to the National Guard, no specific mention was made of this colored company, and the special requirement compelling its organization therefore apparently disappeared from the laws of that state. Finally in 1909 Indiana adopted an act requiring the Adjutant General to organize a battalion of colored infantry as part of the Indiana National Guard.

The value of the colored man as a soldier has long been established. The colored regiments form an effective part of the military organization possessing them. The only question involved in these states was whether the individual colored soldier should be incorporated into a separate regiment or company, or whether he should be distributed throughout the other troops regardless of color. It is not a discrimination, but a matter of some interest to the colored race, to be able to maintain colored regiments, and to prove its efficiency in this respect. Membership in these state troops is voluntary. Such statutes in the Northern states are therefore not discrimination against the negro, but may be called instead a recognition of him.

Discrimination or restriction in jury service has been forbidden by several states, following the example of the Federal Civil Rights law of 1875. The provision of the Federal law is still valid and therefore binding. Nevertheless these states have made the matter doubly sure by adopting specific prohibition of such discrimination on account of color. The states which adopted such a provision were Indiana, Michigan, New Jersey, New York, Ohio, and Rhode Island, the laws all being adopted in 1884 and 1885, except that of New York in 1895.

The testimony of negroes in legal proceedings was specially protected in two states, Washington and West Virginia, which each enacted a provision in 1866 that no one should be incompetent as a witness on account of color. As previously said, no state now prohibits it.

The right to practice law as an attorney was the subject of a special statute in Colorado, which in 1887 provided that no person should be denied such right on account of either race or sex. There had been no previous restriction on account of color, this law being purely protective. In 1870 Iowa specially extended this right to members of all races, it having previously been restricted to white persons.

Legislation concerning suffrage has been referred to in the preceding chapter. It is sufficient to say here that while there has been legislation granting to the negro the right of the ballot, which is there mentioned and will therefore not be repeated in this place, there has been no further legislation concerning this subject which can properly be called protective, with the possible exception of an enactment of New York in 1870, prohibiting any inspector of elections from making any demand of a negro different from that of a white person.

Discrimination in the administration of the charity of any association for the care of orphans was prohibited in an act of Indiana, in 1879, which further provided that associations maintaining colored orphan asylums should be entitled to the allowance provided for in the case of any orphan children. New Jersey in 1853 provided that poor colored servants were to be treated as were white paupers. These were the only examples found of reference to discrimination in the administering of charity or philanthropy.

In the later laws of New York there are several provisions worth comment. In 1899 any discrimination was prohibited against any person or class, in the price charged for admission to any building, park, or other place or enclosure, which was open to the public generally. A statute in 1913 provided with considerable detail that no place of public accommodation or resort should refuse its accommodations to any person, or advertise in any way the fact that such accommodations are refused, on account of race, creed, or color. The production of such communication either written or printed was constituted presumptive violation of the act. Though this statute applied to the negro its passage was supposed to have been secured by the Jewish race, which had been discriminated against in certain cases.

Still another form of statute concerning the colored race was adopted in 1913 in New York, which created an Emancipation

Proclamation Commission to conduct an exhibition and celebration and appropriating $25,000 for this purpose. In 1915 the Governor was authorized to appoint five commissioners for the state of New York to the National Exposition in Richmond in that year to celebrate the same anniversary. In 1915 Illinois also created a commission to conduct an exhibition and celebration in commemoration of the fiftieth anniversary of the emancipation of the negro, appropriating likewise $25,000 for the purpose. These laws while conferring no rights upon the negro, were evidences of the interest in the emancipation of that race felt by the states concerned.

CHAPTER IV

Social Influences Affecting the Legislation

In considering the course of legislation in the different states, is it possible to discover any fundamental underlying causes for the variation in legislation in the several states? Can any principles of action be formulated determining why certain states enact laws restricting the colored race, while other states pass laws to prevent such restriction, and still others ignore the colored question? Is there any reason for a separate education law appearing in a state where no separation in transportation is required, or in another state for intermarriage to be forbidden while separation in education is not required or is even actually prohibited.

In examining the social disturbance created in society by the presence within it of a group dissimilar in nature from the other members, there are several factors to be considered. The effect of such a group will be great or small, and it will be approved or disapproved by the society as a whole, according to the numerical size of the group, according to its dissimilarity from the rest, according to the rapidity of the process of assimilation, according to the strength of the group spirit and group unity, according to the previous spirit of favor or opposition on the part of the other members, according to the activity and aggressiveness of the group, according to its power in controlling the other members and according to the conflict or unity of interest with the other members. This is not meant to be a complete enumeration of all possible factors, but a statement of the more important factors governing the relationship of an alien distinctive group in the midst of a larger social body.

Not all of these factors are of importance in considering the position of the group constituted by the negro race amongst the body of the white population of the various states. The factor of extent of dissimilarity is substantially uniform in the different states. This is not wholly one of social, political and economic ideals, in which regard the negro race has fairly closely approached those members of the white race which occupy a similar social and economic position, but it is also a question of different and distinctive race appearance. The factor of rapidity of assimilation is also substantially uniform throughout the different states, because for the above reason this is chiefly a question of assimilation in race appearance, which is a process of marked slowness, accomplished only through the amalgamation of the races. If all other distinctive characteristics were lost, the difference in race appearance would still suffice to set apart the negro race in a distinct and dissimilar group in a white population, because negro blood is generally easily recognized and complete assimilation is practically impossible for at least several generations.

The factor of group unity is also one which does not greatly affect the treatment of the negro in the different states, for the reason that such group unity is substantially the same everywhere, and further because in fact such unity is inchoate, disorganized, and without adequate expression either for themselves or others. In the past history of the negro race within the United States this factor has at times been one of significance and importance, but it is not at present so.

The factor of the numerical size of the negro group in any state is commonly accepted as the decisive cause for its treatment on the part of the state. Most writers make the simple statement that where the negro race is numerous there it is discriminated against; and where it is small in numbers compared to the rest of the population there it is not a disturbing element, and is either disregarded or else is actively protected. A quotation expressing this view is the following.[1] "The laws and customs of every state in the Union, from the beginning until this good hour, have been influenced by the factor of the relative numerical strength of the negro. . . . In the North he is permitted to attend schools and ride in cars with white people, and is not segregated in theatres, because as yet he is not numerically strong enough to be personally offensive to the white population, or to justify the expense and annoyance which such general separation entails upon the white man himself."

A consideration of the table given at the end of this chapter of the negro population in each state, showing its per cent. as compared with the white population and arrayed in accordance thereto, will make it difficult to accept the theory that the relative numerical strength of the negro in a state determines the treatment accorded

[1] A. H. Stone, *Studies in the American Race Problem*, page 13.

to him by the state. It will be found for example that Washington with a negro population of five-tenths of one per cent. allows intermarriage, having repealed a former law prohibiting it; while Montana with the same per cent. of negro population prohibits intermarriage; as does the state of Idaho which has two-tenths of one per cent., or less than half of the negro population of Washington, its neighboring state. Indiana and Ohio have practically the same per cent. of negroes, yet the former prohibits intermarriage while the latter allows it. New Jersey with three and five-tenths per cent. allows intermarriage, while South Dakota with one-tenth of one per cent. forbids it. The same thing is also seen in considering the states which have enacted Civil Rights laws. There is a group of states in the west, the numbers of whose negro population do not exceed one-tenth of one per cent., which have never enacted any Civil Rights legislation. On the other hand there are a number of the Northern and Eastern states whose per cent. of negro population varies from one per cent. to three and five-tenths per cent., like New Jersey, which have adopted Civil Rights laws. In the same way in considering separation in schools, the fact will be noted that with the exception of the Southern states the numerical factor cannot be discovered as a controlling element.

On the other hand it is plainly evident that the restrictive legislation of the Southern states, which is found in all of them, is due to the very large per cent. of negroes within their borders. Here again however, it becomes evident that this cannot be the sole controlling factor. Kentucky with a little over eleven per cent. and Texas with about eighteen per cent. contain substantially the same restrictive legislation as do the states of South Carolina and Mississippi with over fifty-five per cent. Yet it is evident that the chief difference between the group of Southern states and the other states of the country is found in the large negro population in the former group as a whole.

The relative numerical strength of the negro may accordingly be accepted as a factor, but as only one factor in a situation evidently influenced by other elements. Where there is an overwhelming difference in numerical strength it may cause this factor to be decisive; where there is no overwhelming difference other factors than this are evidently those which control.

The next factor which is of importance to consider is that of the previous attitude of the other members of the population toward the negro group. Here will be found an element which has had an importance only second to that of numbers, in influencing the course of legislation in the different states. In the United States there have been two different forms of opinion in regard to the negro race, the one accustomed to negro slavery and later favoring restriction of the race, the other early opposed to slavery and in favor of abolition, and desiring not only to refrain from imposing restrictions upon the negro, but also actively to protect him and his rights. The one form of opinion and sentiment centered in the South. The other type of opinion had its center in the North, especially in Massachusetts and New York. From the Eastern states both north and south there have flowed forth streams of influence, together with streams of actual emigration, throughout the other states of the union. Those states which were settled largely by Southerners, or which were otherwise in contact with southern influence and connected by economic, social, or other relations with the South, have swung toward the southern type of legislation. Those states which have been largely settled by northern and eastern emigrants or which have been within the predominant sphere of influence of that region have tended to adopt legislation of a corresponding type. When the stream of influence or connection has become weakened through distance or otherwise, as is the case in both regions in certain states, there a partly developed form of legislation appears, similar to its influencing cause but less in volume and weakened in form. Where the streams of northern and southern influence have met in a state and have been in conflict, the legislation concerning the negro will often reflect the conflict, and will indicate which type of influence succeeded in the struggle and finally predominated.

For examples of such cases one may cite such states as Montana, North Dakota, South Dakota and Colorado, which belong to the northern group of states, but whose legislation has been greatly weakened in this respect owing to their geographical distance from the northern center of influence, and the corresponding weakening of the stream. In the same way such states as Arizona and New Mexico show the southern influence, but in a weakened form. New Mexico being located close to a third focus of influence, namely,

Mexico, affords an example of the early southern influence having been overcome by the effects of the influence of the population of Mexican blood. In such states as Kansas one can see the struggle for predominance between northern and southern influence, the northern predominating but not quite completely. Both Indiana and Ohio show in their legislation the results of southern immigration entering the southern portions of the state and in conflict with northern immigration coming largely into the northern portion of the states. Ohio, however, has become a typical northern state, while Indiana still shows traces of its southern influence, as evidenced in its permissive separate school law and in its law against intermarriage, such laws in Ohio having appeared earlier in its history but later having entirely disappeared.

It must be recognized therefore that this factor of the traditional attitude toward the negro group of the other portion of the population is of almost equal weight with that of relative numerical strength.

Beside these two factors there is also a third one whose importance has not often been recognized. This is the factor of the power possessed by the negro group. Such power in a democracy is not expressed in terms of physical or military strength but in terms of political influence.

In the Southern states the negroes did not possess the right of suffrage, until this was conferred upon them in form by the Fifteenth Amendment in 1870. The actual effect of this amendment was not to place the actual ballot in the hand of every negro. At no time in the history of these states, except briefly and in limited form during Reconstruction, has the negro race been in a position to enforce its desires at the polls. This result has been accomplished in part through the moral ascendancy of the white race over the colored race exercised to limit its use of the ballot, in part by such restrictions in the election laws as tend to disenfranchise negroes more than whites, and at times by other measures. The large group of the colored race in the South since Reconstruction days has therefore been in a position where it possessed no great power of the only kind which is effective. As a result, there has been no need to seek to secure their favorable consideration for any measure or for any party.

On the other hand, in the Northern states since 1870 the negro has everywhere received the ballot upon terms of equality with the white race. The result of this is that where his numbers have been large enough in the community, it has been of importance to the political managers of the different political groups to consult his interests and to endeavor to secure his cooperation. The effect of this is to reverse the influence of the relative numerical strength of the colored race. In the South numerical strength acts to handicap the negro and to increase discriminations against him in legislation. In the Northern states where the negro is weak in numbers, he is thereby weak in political influence. Where he is strong in numbers he becomes strong in political influence. In some states his aid and support is actively sought at election time. The great political parties take pains to plan measures for securing his allegiance and his favor. Such statutes as those of New York and Illinois creating an emancipation proclamation commission to celebrate the fiftieth anniversary of emancipation, show not only a friendly interest in the colored race, but also reflect a desire on the part of the party in power to win his political support. The negro population of the two cities of Chicago and New York, which is large enough to be of marked importance at election time, was a factor in the case of each of these statutes.

Where the negro has once secured the ballot it may prove a matter of difficulty to withdraw it from him again. This has been the history of the extension of the right of suffrage. Once conferred, it is only with difficulty withdrawn. This will probably lead, as the negro numbers of the Northern states increase, to the repeal of some of the existing restrictions affecting him, and to the enactment of further laws in his favor, if he feels such are desirable. If the negro race in the South should come into the full exercise of the franchise it would probably be followed by alterations in the present southern legislation.

The further factor of the aggressiveness of the group concerned is not of much importance in considering the negro problem. Nowhere is the negro at present aggressive politically. He is inclined to be docile to those whom he recognizes as leaders. He shows little of the political talent or aptitude, for example, of the Irish race. If the negro were to become more active politically, or if he were directed by political leaders able to maintain a close group unity and to direct aggressively along political lines, the negro would probably secure more political recognition than he has as yet. There is one possible alternative to this, in that the present comparative inactivity of the negro politically disarms any hostility which might otherwise be aroused on the part of the white race if the negro becomes too aggressive before his numbers become such that no white political leader or party can afford to oppose him. As has just been said, however, the position of those writers is probably wrong who hold that an increased number of negroes in the Northern states will automatically lead to hostility and opposition by the mere force of the fact of such numbers. On the contrary, their increase may result in increased consideration and in strengthened position, unless the varying white interests should be united into a compact force directed against the colored race. As the negro in the North increases in numbers it will not necessarily prove true that proportionate discrimination against him will arise.

There is another element which enters into the question of the effect on legislation in the different states of the factors which have just been considered. The different subjects of legislation are not equally affected by any single factor of those mentioned. Certain lines of legislation are more responsive to relative numerical strength, while others are affected more by other elements. For example, separation in transportation is obviously more connected with the numbers of the negro race in the population, or to be more accurate, their numbers in the travelling portion of the population. Yet this also is subject to modification through the operation of other factors. Oklahoma with a comparatively small negro population required separation in the waiting rooms of all railway stations throughout the state. It was later found necessary to modify this, as many small places in the state had no negroes whatever and it was impossible to maintain separate waiting rooms which would never be used. The law against intermarriage is not greatly affected by the numerical strength of the negro. Its adoption evidently depends upon the strength of the sentiment against racial admixture, without primary reference to the volume of the colored race in the state. Statutes in restriction of the colored race may be ranked in accordance with the tendency toward their adoption. The law against intermarriage is not only usually the first to appear chronologically, but is also the most widespread. Next comes separation in education, following that, separation in transportation, and thereafter miscellaneous minor provisions.

In considering the laws of the Northern states in protection of the colored race, the factors above referred to can be seen in operation in a more limited way. The relative numerical strength of the colored race plays no part whatever in securing the adoption of a Civil Rights law, except, as would be expected, by reverse effect. That is, the states located in the North which have the largest proportion of the colored race have all adopted Civil Rights statutes. Those states which have not yet enacted such legislation are the states where the colored population is very small in proportion.

The traditional attitude of the white portion of the population is of more importance in determining the adoption of Civil Rights laws. Where the state has been in the direct line of Northern influence there such legislation appears. This factor is the controlling one in most of the Northern states, in the adoption of such legislation, rather than any of the others. It is this factor also which, as has been indicated, has led to the repealing of earlier restrictive laws in the Northern states. This has been done in spite of the steadily increasing numbers of the colored population of those states.

The factor of conflict of interest must finally be considered. This interest will in most cases be economic. It can arise, however, from such motives as religion, nationality, and lesser causes. For example, a group otherwise almost identical with the general body may be led by reasons of nationality into hostility with it, as seen in the case of Germans long resident in England but for the duration of the war necessarily interned to protect the nation. The factor of conflict of interest affects the negro at present only slightly, and that through the side of economic interest. It has future possibilities, however, both in the North and in the South, especially because of the influx of negro laborers into the North. If negro workingmen come into active competition with white workingmen over securing of available work, or other industrial interests, it will carry the possibility of arousing active hostility. This will arise more easily and be more active on account of the negro dissimilarity. There is in this factor the possibility of a reversal of the course of legislation in the North concerning the negro. It is not yet active. Whether it will arise cannot now be foreseen.

To sum up briefly, there are a number of factors whose operation determines the passage of legislation either in the protection of or in restriction of the negro. They are somewhat affected by the varying resisting powers of the different types of legislation. These factors seem intelligibly and sufficiently to explain not only present legislation but also the historical development through which it has passed.

As a result of the operation of these factors, the different states can be classified into various groups, according to the attitude of their legislation toward the negro race. It is apparent that the Southern states form one group. Within this group there are slight differences, some states being leaders in the development of certain legislation, and some showing slightly different tendencies from the others. These differences while distinct are not marked enough to warrant splitting up the Southern states into sub-groups. Various minor classifications and divisions can be made through examination of the laws and their development, as found in these states, but such differences are not sufficient to create any great distinction among the Southern states. Missouri alone constitutes an exception, showing strong northern influence.

The state of New Mexico must be placed in a classification by itself. Its legislation was at first southern in tendency. This influence was later overcome, as seen elsewhere, not by northern influence but by the influence of the Mexican population of the state. The state therefore should not be grouped with either Northern or Southern states, but forms a distinct division, although but a single state. It will be noted that the other states bordering upon the Mexican frontier have not been affected in the same manner and fall into the other classifications herein referred to.

The Northern states as a whole may be regarded as a distinct group in themselves. There are evident among them, however, distinctly marked differences which require their further classification into sub-groups.

The first of these sub-groups to require attention is that consisting of the border states of the North in proximity to the Southern states. These border states distinctly show the results of this proximity. Either in their present legislation or in their past legislation, they are distinct from the other Northern states. This can be recognized in Ohio, Indiana, Kansas and other states. It does not hold, however, for all of the states just north of the border. In Pennsylvania, unlike the situation in Ohio, Indiana and Illinois,

Southern influence did not penetrate through the southern portion of the state sufficiently to reach the legislative centres.

The states which lie at the point of furthest distance from the Southern states again form a somewhat distinct group by themselves. They are isolated by reason of their position from participation in the negro question, regardless of other factors. An example of this can be seen in New England, where the southern New England states are typically northern states. The northern New England states of Maine, New Hampshire and Vermont are entirely distinct in their legislative attitude from the southern section of New England. The stream of influence affecting such legislation which flowed from Massachusetts evidently tended southward and westward. The northern New England States were left in an eddy of the stream, and remained unaffected by its current. They also may be said to have been separated by buffer states, the southern New England states serving this purpose. Further west similar states located upon the northern border can be recognized, which likewise have been isolated from lively participation in the negro problem by the other Northern states lying between themselves and the South. Montana and North Dakota are in this group, and one or two others should perhaps also be placed in it.

The Western states as a whole, omitting the tier of states immediately to the west of the Mississippi River, while entirely Northern in their main classification, form roughly a group by themselves, in that they show weakened Northern influence and a distinct admixture of Southern influence. The legislation in this group of states varies from state to state. One cannot generalize, as can be done in those states of the Northern group which lie further east, as to what precise forms of legislation exist in them. These states then form a somewhat distinct group, not so much owing to the strong predominance of a given type of legislation, as owing to the absence of this.

The remaining Northern group of states is of course that group in the east and the middle west which are in every respect strong typical Northern states. These sub-groups within the larger Northern group will be seen to be in accordance with the operation of the principles which have just been discussed, and to yield further illustrations of their operation.

The most typical Southern law, which is found in every state within the Southern group, with the exception of Missouri and Delaware, is the law requiring separation in transportation. Civil Rights legislation has commonly been regarded as the distinctive mark of Northern states. This is not the case. Many of the Northern states which are in no respect whatever influenced by the South do not possess such a law. The Northern states are marked rather by absence of Southern influence, and by various laws of Northern trend.

While statesmen and observers of public affairs have devoted great attention to the many different sides of the negro question, there can be found little evidence in statutory enactments that legislators have done likewise. In the South, the one underlying motive of separation has been the controlling force. In the North, attention has been paid chiefly to protecting the interests and rights of the negro from invasion, with the addition of a few scattered restrictive measures. The legislation shows no constructive plans and measures for the development and welfare of the colored race, either in the North or in the South. The single exception to this is an abortive and fruitless colonization plan. Various plans for the development of the colored race socially and economically have been proposed, and one might expect in the history of legislation especially in the South a record of experiments in such lines. Social experimentation is constantly being carried on through legislation on many subjects of the public welfare. None of this is found with reference to the negro.

One reason for this lies in the fact that it is in large part impossible to enact legislation directed specially and solely toward the negro race, even for the development and welfare of that race. Legislation must today apply to both races without discrimination. Further, many measures of social construction may in fact benefit the negro, and whatever enactments make for the welfare of the white population or of the general population should also make for the welfare of the negro. Through separate institutions and educational facilities, and in other ways, various constructive measures are in fact being developed outside the field of legislation.

To what extent legislation can be utilized as a constructive force in solving the negro problem, however, lies outside the scope of this essay. It need only be remarked, in closing, that it has not been so utilized to the extent that would seem to have been possible.

TABLES

Tables showing chronological enactment of legislation
  Acts concerning intermarriage
  Acts sanctioning separation in education
  Acts prohibiting separation in education
  Acts concerning transportation
  Acts concerning civil rights
Table of the number and per cent. of negro population in each state.

DESCRIPTION

In each table of legislation the italic abbreviation of a state, thus, *Mass.*, signifies the original legislation in that state concerning the given subject. Where the abbreviation of a state is not in italics, it signifies further enactments after the original act.

The table concerning intermarriage shows the legislation on this subject, the names of states with no description following signifying legislation prohibiting intermarriage. Legislation is not included which consists of repetition in compiled statutes or otherwise of previous acts.

The table of legislation sanctioning separation in education shows the legislation approving of such separation, whether permissive or compulsory. Absence of description signifies compulsory legislation, other forms being named. Legislation referring to private schools or schools other than public is so described.

The table of legislation prohibiting separation in education contains the laws of that nature, the insertion of them in the preceding table being found undesirable.

The table of legislation concerning transportation contains the laws on that subject. Where not specified the laws are requirements of separation in the cars of railroads.

The table of legislation concerning civil rights shows the laws referring to that subject. When not described, the laws establish civil rights. Other legislation is described.

CHRONOLOGICAL RECORD OF LEGISLATION CONCERNING INTERMARRIAGE

Laws other than prohibition of intermarriage are indicated

1786 *Mass.*
1798 *R. I.*
1821 *Me.*
1834 Mass.
1838 *Mich.*
1843 *Ind.*, Mass. (repeal).
1850 *Cal.*
1852
1854 *Wash.*
1855 *Kan.*
1857 Me. (omit), *N. Mex.*
1859 Kan. (repeal).
1861 *Nev.*, *Ohio.*
1862 *Ore.*
1864 *Colo.*
1865 *Ariz.*, Ga., Miss., *S. C.*, Wash., Ala. (Constitution).
1866 *Neb.*, N. Mex. (repeal), Ark., Mo., Ky.
1867 *Ida.*, Wash. (repeal), Ore.
1868 S. C. (repeal).
1870 Tenn. (Constitution, statute).
1871 Miss. (omitted).
1872 R. I. (repeated), Ala. (law held void by state court).
1873 Va., N. C.
1874 Del.
1875 N. C. (Constitution).
1877 Ala. (law again held valid by state court).
1879 S. C. (reenacted), Tex.
1880 Miss. (inserted).
1881 Fla., R. I. (repealed).
1882 *W. Va.*
1883 Me. (repealed), Mich. (repealed).
1884 Md.
1885 Neb.
1887 Ohio (repealed).
1888 *Utah.*
1890 Miss. (Constitution).
1894 *La.*
1895 S. C. (Constitution).
1901 Ala.
1907 *Okla.*
1908 La. (concubinage).
1909 *Mont.*, *S. Dak.*
1913 Neb., S. Dak.

CHRONOLOGICAL RECORD OF LEGISLATION SANCTIONING SEPARATION IN EDUCATION

Laws other than separation laws are indicated

1829 *Ohio.*
1843 *Ind.* (permit).
1845 *La.* (Constitution), N. Y. (local), Va.
1846 *Iowa*, *Mo.* (not to teach).
1847 Ohio (permit).
1852 *Del.*, Ohio (require), N. Y. (local).
1854 *Pa.*
1858 Iowa (held unconstitutional by court, 1858).
1862 *Kan.*
1864 N. Y. (general, permit).
1865 Mo., Mo. (Constitution), *Nev.*, *W. Va.*
1866 *Ark.*, *Tenn.*, *Tex.*
1868 *Ala.*, Kan. (permit).
1869 *Cal.*, Ind., Pa. (local), Va., *Ky.* (permit).
1870 *Md.*, Tenn. (Constitution).
1871 *Mont.*
1872 *Ga.*, Md., Pa. (repeal of 1869 law), W. Va. (Constitution).
1873 Ark., Ky. (general), Nev. (omitted).
1875 *N. C.* (Constitution), Ala., (Constitution).
1876 Kan., Tex. (Constitution).
1877 Ind. (permit), Ga. (Constitution). Del.
1878 *Miss.*, Ohio (permit).
1880 Cal. (repeal).
1881 Pa. (repeal of general law of 1854).
1883 Del.
1885 Fla. (Constitution), N. C.
1887 Ohio (repeal), *Wyo.* (permit).
1889 Mont. (omit).
1890 Miss. (Constitution), *Okla.* (permit).
1891 Ky. (Constitution).
1893 Del., Tex.
1895 Ga., Fla. (private schools), S. C. (Constitution), Tex.
1896 S. C.
1897 Okla.
1898 Del., La. (Constitution).
1900 N. Y. (repeal and prohibited).
1901 Ala., Tenn. (private schools).
1902 Va. (Constitution).
1903 N. C.
1904 Ky. (private schools).
1905 Kan.
1907 Okla. (Constitution).
1908 Okla. (private schools).
1909 *Ariz.* (permit).
1913 Fla.

CHRONOLOGICAL RECORD OF LEGISLATION PROHIBITING SEPARATION IN EDUCATION

Laws other than prohibition of separation are indicated

1855	*Mass.*
1857	*Iowa.*
1868	*La.* (Constitution), *S. C.* (Constitution).
1871	*Mich.*
1873	*N. Y.* (in Civil Rights law).
1874	*Ill.*, *Kan.* (in Civil Rights law).
1876	*Colo.* (Constitution), Kan. (by omission).
1877	*Minn.*
1879	La. (Constitution omit).
1881	Kan., *N. J.*, *Pa.*
1882	*R. I.*
1889	*Ida.*, *Mont.* (Constitution).
1895	Utah (Constitution), Mont.
1900	N.Y. (full prohibition law).
1901	*Ariz.*, *N. Mex.*
1903	N. J.
1905	Minn.
1909	Ariz. (repeal by permissive law).
1911	N. Mex. (Constitution).

CHRONOLOGICAL RECORD OF LEGISLATION CONCERNING SEPARATION IN TRANSPORTATION

Laws other than requirements of separation are indicated

NOTE. Prohibition of separation when merely a clause in a civil rights statute is not recorded here, except for the first provision, in Massachusetts, and for the Southern states, otherwise most of the civil rights laws would necessarily be here included.

1865 *Fla.*, *Miss.*, Mass. (prohibited in Civil Rights law).
1866 *Tex.*
1867 Pa. (prohibited).
1869 La. (prohibited), Miss. (prohibited in Constitution).
1870 Ga. (prohibited).
1871 Tex. (prohibited in Civil Rights law).
1873 Miss. (prohibited in Civil Rights law), La. (prohibited in Civil Rights law), Ark. (prohibited in Civil Rights law), Fla. (prohibited in Civil Rights law).
1875 Del. (permitted, cars and boats), Tenn. (permitted).
1881 *Tenn.*
1882 Tenn.
1887 *Fla.*
1888 *Miss.* (also authorized in depots).
1889 *Tex.*
1890 *La.*
1891 *Ala.*, *Ark.*, Tenn., Tex., *Ga.* (also partial street railway requirement).
1892 *Ky.*
1893 Ark. (waiting rooms also), Ky.
1894 La. (depots).
1898 *S. C.*
1899 Ga., *N. C.*
1900 S. C., *Va.*
1901 N. C., Va. (partial street railway law).
1902 La. (street railways), Va. (partial street railways).
1903 Ark. (street railways), S. C., Tenn. (partial street railways).
1904 *Md.*, Miss. (street railways), S. C., Va. (depots, wharves authorized), Md. (boats).
1905 Fla. (street railways), S. C. (suburban railways), Tenn. (street railways).
1906 S. C. (meals at depots), Va. (street railways, general).
1907 Fla. (waiting rooms, electric cars), N. C. (street railways), *Okla.*, Okla. (street railways and depots), Tex. (street railways).
1908 Md. (electric railways), Md. (railroads and boats).
1909 Tex. (depots).
1911 Okla.

CHRONOLOGICAL RECORD OF LEGISLATION CONCERNING CIVIL RIGHTS

(Including also life insurance acts)

Laws other than requirement of civil rights are indicated

1865 *Mass.*, Mo. (Constitution), United States (Thirteenth Amendment).

1866 Mass., Fla. (Anti-Civil Rights), United States.

1868 *S. C.* (Constitution), United States (Fourteenth Amendment).

1869 *La.*, S. C.

1870 United States (Fifteenth Amendment), United States (Enforcement Act).

1871 *Tex.*

1873 *Ark.*, Del. (Anti-Civil Rights), La., *Fla.*, *Miss.*, *N. Y.*

1874 *Kan.*

1875 Del. (Anti-Civil Rights), Tenn. (Anti-Civil Rights), United States.

1876 N. C. (Anti-Civil Rights).

1881 N. Y.

1883 (United States Civil Rights cases).

1884 *Conn.*, *Iowa*, Mass. (life insurance), *N. J.*, *Ohio*.

1885 *Colo.*, *Ill.*, *Ind.*, Mass., *Mich.*, *Minn.*, *Neb.*, *R. I.*

1887 Conn. (life insurance), *Pa.*

1889 Conn. (life insurance), Ohio (life insurance), *Wash.*

1891 Ill., N. Y. (life insurance).

1892 Iowa.

1893 *Cal.*, Mass., Mich. (life insurance), Neb., Ohio (life insurance).

1894 Ohio.

1895 Colo., Mass., N. Y., Wash., *Wisc.*

1897 Cal., Ill., Minn.

1898 N. J.

1899 Minn., N. Y.

1902 La. (repeal).

1903 Ill.

1905 Conn.

1907 Ark. (repeal).

1909 Wash.

1911 Ill.

1913 N. Y.

ABSOLUTE NUMBERS AND PER CENT. OF NEGRO POPULATION IN EACH STATE

United States Census of 1910

1	N. H.	564	.1	26	Ill.	109,049	1.9
2	Wis.	2,900	.1	27	Ind.	60,320	2.2
3	N. Dak.	617	.1	28	Ohio	111,452	2.3
4	S. Dak.	817	.1	29	Pa.	193,919	2.5
5	Me.	1,363	.2	30	Kans.	54,030	3.2
6	Ida.	651	.2	31	N. J.	89,760	3.5
7	Ore.	1,492	.2	32	Mo.	157,452	4.8
8	Minn.	7,084	.3	33	W. Va.	64,173	5.3
9	Utah	1,144	.3	34	Okla.	137,612	8.3
10	Vt.	1,621	.5	35	Ky.	261,656	11.4
11	Mont.	1,834	.5	36	Del.	31,181	15.4
12	N. Mex.	1,628	.5	37	Tex.	690,049	17.7
13	Wash.	6,058	.5	38	Md.	232,250	17.9
14	Mich.	17,115	.6	39	Tenn.	473,088	21.7
15	Neb.	7,689	.6	40	Ark.	442,891	28.1
16	Nev.	513	.6	41	D. C.	94,446	28.5
17	Ia.	14,973	.7	42	N. C.	697,843	31.6
18	Cal.	21,645	.9	43	Va.	671,096	32.6
19	Ariz.	2,009	1.0	44	Fla.	308,669	41.0
20	Mass.	38,055	1.1	45	Ala.	908,282	42.5
21	Conn.	15,174	1.4	46	La.	713,874	43.1
22	Colo.	11,453	1.4	47	Ga.	1,176,987	45.1
23	N. Y.	134,191	1.5	48	S. C.	835,843	55.2
24	Wyo.	2,235	1.5	49	Miss.	1,009,487	56.2
25	R. I.	9,529	1.8				
					Total	9,827,763	

PART II

CHRONOLOGICAL RECORD OF THE LAWS

United States

1856

Dred Scott v. Sandford, 19 Howard (United States), p. 393, 1856. The decision delivered by Chief Justice Taney held that persons of the African race who were brought to the country, together with their descendants, were chattels with "no rights and privileges but such as those who hold the power and conduct the government might choose to grant them," and that they were not citizens nor capable of being such.

1865

Amendment XIII, 13 Stat. L., p. 567, Feb. 1, 1865. Section 1. Neither slavery nor involuntary servitude, except as a punishment for crime whereof the party shall have been duly convicted, shall exist within the United States, or any place subject to their jurisdiction. (Proclamation of ratification, December 18, 1865.)

1866

14 Stat. L., p. 27, April 9, 1866. An act to protect all persons in the United States in their Civil Rights.

Section 1. All persons born in the United States and not subject to any foreign power, excluding Indians not taxed, are hereby declared to be citizens of the United States, and such citizens of every race and color, without regard to any previous condition of slavery or involuntary servitude, except as a punishment for a crime whereof the party shall have been duly convicted, shall have the same right, in every State and Territory in the United States, to make and enforce contracts, to sue, be parties, and give evidence, to inherit, purchase, lease, sell, hold, and convey real and personal property, and to full and equal benefit of all laws and proceedings for security of person and property, as is enjoyed by white citizens, and shall be subject to like punishment, pains, and penalties, and to none other, any law, statute, ordinance, regulation or custom, to the contrary notwithstanding.

Section 2. Any person who under color of any law, statute, ordinance, regulation or custom, shall subject, or cause to be subjected, any inhabitant of any State or Territory to the deprivation of any right secured or protected by this act, or to different punishment, pains, or penalty, on account of such person having at any time been in a condition of slavery or involuntary servitude or by reason of his color or race, than is prescribed for the punishment of white persons, is guilty of a misdemeanor and may be fined not exceeding $1,000, or imprisoned not exceeding one year, or both.

Amendment XIV, 14 Stat. L., p. 358, June 16, 1866. Section 1. All persons born or naturalized in the United States and subject to the jurisdiction thereof are citizens of the United States, and of the State wherein they reside. No State shall make or enforce any law which shall abridge the privileges or immunities of citizens of the United States; nor shall any State deprive any person of life, liberty, or property without due process of law, nor deny to any person within its jurisdiction the equal protection of the laws. (Proclamation of ratification, July 28, 1868.)

1869

Amendment XV, 15 Stat. L., p. 346, February 27, 1869. The right of any citizens of the United States to vote shall not be denied or abridged by the United States or by any State on account of race, color or previous condition of servitude. (Proclamation of ratification, March 30, 1870.)

1870

16 Stat. L., p. 140. Enforcement Act. Approved May 31, 1870. Act to enforce the Rights of Citizens of the United States to vote in the several States, and for other purposes.

Section 1. Race, color or previous condition of servitude shall not affect the right to vote at any election.

Section 2. Nor shall the enforcement of any prerequisite to the right of voting affect such right. Penalty, $500 forfeit to the person aggrieved, with full costs and allowance for counsel fees, and the offender shall be guilty of a misdemeanor, with a fine of not less than $500 or imprisonment from one month to one year, or both.

Section 4. Penalty for unlawfully obstructing any citizen from qualifying himself to vote, or from voting, a fine of not more than $500 or imprisonment from one month to one year, or both.

Section 5. Intimidating or attempting to intimidate by bribery or threats from exercising right of suffrage; same penalty.

Section 16. All persons shall have same right to make and enforce contracts, to sue, be parties, give evidence, and to the full and equal benefit of all laws and proceedings for security of person and property as is enjoyed by white citizens, and shall be subject to like punishment, pains, penalties, taxes, licenses, and exactions of every kind, and none other, any law, statute, ordinance, regulation or custom, to the contrary notwithstanding; and any law of any State in conflict with this provision is hereby declared null and void.

Section 17. Penalty, a fine not exceeding $1,000 or imprisonment not exceeding one year, or both.

Section 18. The Act to protect all persons in United States in their Civil Rights and to furnish the means of their vindication, passed April 9, 1866, is hereby reenacted, and sections 16 and 17 hereof shall be enforced according to the provisions of said Act.

1871

17 Stat. L., p. 13, April 20, 1871. Act to enforce Provisions of Fourteenth Amendment, and for other purposes.

Section 1. Any person who under color of any law, statute, ordinance, regulation, custom, or usage of any state, shall subject or cause to be subjected, any person within the jurisdiction of the United States to the deprivation of any rights, privileges or immunities secured by the Constitution of the United States, shall, any such law to the contrary notwithstanding, be liable to the party injured in any action at law, etc.

Penalty, a fine from $500 to $5,000, or imprisonment with or without hard labor from six months to six years, or both.

1875

18 Stat. L., p. 335, March 1, 1875. Act to protect all citizens in their civil and legal rights.

Section 1. Whereas it is essential to just government that we recognize the equality of all men before the law, and hold that it is the duty of government in its dealings with people to mete out equal and exact justice to all, of whatever nationality, race, color or persuasion, religious or political; and it being the appropriate object of legislation to enact great fundamental principles into law; Therefore, be it enacted, etc. That all persons within the jurisdiction of the United States shall be entitled to full and equal enjoyment of the accommodations, advantages, facilities and privileges of inns, public conveyances on land or water, theaters, and other places of public amusement; subject only to the conditions and limitations established by law and applicable alike to citizens of every race and color, regardless of any previous condition of servitude.

Section 2. For the denial of such rights except for reasons by law applicable to citizens of every race and color, and regardless of any previous condition of servitude, or for aiding or inciting such denials, the offender shall forfeit and pay the sum of $500 to the person aggrieved, with full costs, and upon conviction he shall be deemed guilty of a misdemeanor and fined not less than $500 nor more than $1,000, or shall be imprisoned from thirty days to one year. Provided that all persons may elect to sue for the penalty aforesaid or to proceed under their rights at common law and by State statutes, and having elected to proceed in the one mode or the other, their right to proceed in the other jurisdiction shall be barred. But this proviso shall not apply to criminal proceedings, either under this act or the criminal law of any State. Provided further, That a judgment for the penalty in favor of the party aggrieved or a judgment upon an indictment, shall be a bar to either prosecution respectively.

Section 4. No citizen possessing all other qualifications which are or may be prescribed by law shall be disqualified for service as grand or petit juror in any Court of United States, or of any State, on account of race, color, or previous condition of servitude; and any officer or other person charged with any duty in the selection or summoning of jurors who shall exclude or fail to summon any citizen for the cause aforesaid shall, on conviction thereof, be deemed guilty of misdemeanor, and be fined not more than $5,000.

1883

Civil Rights Cases, 109 United States, p. 3, 1883. Five cases brought on account of violation of Civil Rights, in Kansas, California, Missouri, New York, and Tennessee.

Judge Bradley. "These cases are all founded on the first and second sections of the Act of Congress, known as the Civil Rights Act, passed March 1, 1875. Two of the cases are for denying to persons of color the accommodations and privileges of any inn or hotel; two of them are, the one for denying the privileges and accommodations of a theater—in refusing a colored person a seat in the dress circle, and the other for denying the full enjoyment of the accommodations of the theater known as the Grand Opera House in New York, said denial not being made for any reasons by law applicable to citizens of every race and color, and regardless of any previous condition of servitude; the last case on account of the refusal of the conductor of a railroad company to allow the wife of complainant to ride in a ladies car for the reason that she was a person of African descent."

"The primary and important question in all the cases is the constitutionality of the law. No one will contend that the power to pass it was contained in the Constitution before the adoption of the last three amendments."

Concerning the Fourteenth Amendment, the Court held, "It is State action of a particular character that is prohibited. Individual invasion of individual rights is not the subject matter of the amendment." "It does not authorize Congress to create a code of municipal law for the regulation of private rights, but to provide modes of redress against the operation of State laws, and the action of State officers, executive or judicial, when these are subversive of the fundamental rights specified in the Amendment." "And so in the present case, until some State law has been passed or some State action has been taken, no legislation of the United States can be called into activity. Of course, legislation may be provided in advance to meet the exigency when it arises, but not general legislation upon the rights of the citizen, but corrective legislation."

Concerning the Thirteenth Amendment the Court held, "Can the act of a mere individual, the owner of the inn, the public conveyance, or place of amusement, refusing the accommodation, be justly regarded as imposing any badge of slavery or servitude upon the applicant, or only as inflicting an ordinary civil injury, properly cognizable by the laws of the State, and presumably subject to redress by those laws until the contrary appears?" "We are forced to the conclusion that such an act of refusal has nothing to do with slavery or involuntary servitude, and that if it is violative of any right of the party, his redress is to be sought under the laws of the State; or if those laws are adverse to his rights and do not protect him, his remedy will be found in the corrective legislation which Congress has adopted or may adopt for counteracting the effect of State laws or State action, prohitited by the Fourteenth Amendment."

"The first and second sections of the Act are unconstitutional and void."

An able dissenting opinion by Judge Harlan supported the Act under the Thirteenth Amendment, which he held established and decreed universal civil freedom throughout the United States. He also held that the Fourteenth Amendment gave Congress power to enforce an express prohibition upon the States. The rights which Congress by the Act of 1875 sought to secure were legal, not social, rights.

Alabama

1865

Penal Code, 1865–1866. Sections 61, 62. Any white person and any negro, or descendant of any negro to third generation, inclusive, though one ancestor of each generation was a white person, intermarrying or committing adultery, or fornication, shall each be punished by imprisonment not less than two years nor more than seven years. Penalty for issuing the license or performing the ceremony shall be a fine of from $100 to $1,000 or also imprisonment not more than six months. (See Criminal Code, 1852, Section 61.)

Constitution, 1865, Article IV. Section 31. It shall be the duty of the general assembly at its next session, and from time to time thereafter, to enact laws prohibiting the intermarriage of white with negro persons, or with persons of mixed blood, declaring such marriages null and void *ab initio*, and fixing penalties.

Constitution, 1865, Article IV. Section 36. The general assembly shall enact such laws at its next session, and from time to time thereafter, as will protect the freedmen of the State, and guard them and the State against evils that may arise from their sudden emancipation.

Laws, 1865–1866, p. 98. Witnesses. Negroes shall testify only in open court, and only when a freed man, free negro, or a mulatto is a party.

1866

Code, 1867, p. 64. All marriages between freed men and freed women, during slavery or after, solemnized by persons having or claiming authority, shall be valid if parties are still living together.

1867

Constitution, 1867, Article VII. Section 2. Removed the limitation of the vote to whites.

Revised Code, 1867, Sections 3602 and 3603. If a white person and a negro, descended from negro ancestors to the third generation inclusive though one ancestor in each generation may have been white, shall intermarry, or live in adultery or fornication, they shall be punished by confinement in the penitentiary at hard labor for not less than two years nor more than seven years. Knowingly issuing the license or performing the ceremony shall be punished by a fine from $100 to $1,000, or imprisonment for six months, or both. (See Code, 1852, Section 1946.)

1868

Laws, 1868, p. 148. It is not lawful to unite in one school colored and white children, unless by unanimous consent of parents and guardians. Trustees shall in all other cases provide separate schools.

1872

Burns v. State, 48 Alabama, p. 195, 1872. Sections 3602 and 3603 of the Revised Code, prohibiting intermarriage of white persons and negroes, were held to be in contravention to the Civil Rights Bill of April 9, 1866, and repugnant to the Fourteenth Amendment, Section 1. The Court held that marriage is a civil contract and the same right to make a contract as is enjoyed by white citizens, means the right to make any contract which a white citizen may make.

1873

Laws, 1873, p. 179. A free normal school for colored teachers established at Huntsville.

Laws, 1873, p. 176. Provided for a "State Normal School and University" for the Colored Race, for the education of colored teachers and students (at Marion), upon most approved plan, and in connection therewith a university department to provide for the liberal education of the colored race in the same manner as was already provided for the education of the white race in our universities and colleges.

1875

Constitution, Article I. Section 38. There shall be no education or property qualification for suffrage or for office; nor any restraint upon the same on account of race, color, or previous condition of servitude, shall be made by law.

Constitution, Article XIII. Section 1. Separate schools shall be provided for the children of citizens of African descent.

1876

Laws, 1876, p. 285. White and negro prisoners are not to be confined permanently together in the same apartments before conviction, if there are enough separate apartments. Misdemeanor, with a penalty of a fine not less than $50 nor more than $100.

Laws, 1876, p. 98. Section 9. Poll Tax. Names of tax-payers of colored race are to be kept in separate books. Amounts paid by persons of colored race shall be devoted to maintenance of schools for the colored race.

1877

Green v. State. 58 Alabama 190 (1877). Overruling Burns v. State, 1872. The law against white persons and negroes intermarrying was held to be a valid law. The Court held that marriage is not a mere contract, but a social or domestic institution. The law declared to be a punishable offense a marriage *between* a white person and a negro. And it no more tolerated it in one of the parties than in the other. There was no discrimination made in favor of the white person.

1878

Laws 1878, p. 136. Repeated separate school requirement of 1875 Constitution.

1884–1885

Laws 1884–1885, p. 192. It is unlawful for white convicts, whether state or county convicts, and colored convicts to be chained together, or to be allowed to sleep together, or to be confined in same room or apartment when not at work.

Laws 1884–1885, p. 349. Repeated separate school provision.

1891

Laws, 1891, p. 412. All railroads carrying passengers, other than street railways, shall provide equal but separate accommodations for the white and colored races, by providing two or more passenger cars for each passenger train, or by dividing the passenger cars by partitions so as to secure separate accommodations.

Section 2. The conductor is to assign each passenger to his place. If a passenger refuses to occupy it, he may refuse to carry such passenger on train, and is not liable for damages. But this section does not apply to white or colored passengers entering the state upon railroads under contract for transportation made in other states where like laws to this do not prevail.

Section 3. A person riding or attempting to ride in wrong place in railroad coach, is subject to a fine of $100.

Section 4. All railroad companies neglecting to comply with the requirements of this act within sixty days, shall be guilty of a misdemeanor, and fined not exceeding $500. Any conductor, etc., neglecting to carry out the provisions of the act, is guilty of a misdemeanor, and may be fined an amount not to exceed $100. (Code, 1907, Section 5487, Section 7684.)

1896

Code, 1896. Sections 3607–3608. Colored poll taxes shall go to the support of colored schools.

Code, 1896. Section 3720. Alabama School for Negro Deaf and Blind established.

1901

Constitution, 1901, Article IV. Section 102. The legislature shall never pass any law to authorize or legalize any marriage between any white person and a negro, or descendant of a negro.

1901

Constitution, 1901, Article XIV. Section 256. Separate schools shall be provided for white and colored children, and no child of either race shall be permitted to attend a school of the other race.

1907

Code, 1907, I. Section 1757. Schools. Separate school requirement repeated.

Code, 1907, I. Section 1858. Negro taxes are to be kept separate.

Criminal Code, 1907. Section 7421. Any white person and any negro, or any descendant of any negro to the third generation inclusive, though one ancestor of each generation was a white person, if they intermarry or commit adultery or fornication, shall each be punished by imprisonment of not less than two years nor more than seven years.

Any officer knowingly issuing a license for such marriage, or any person knowingly performing the ceremony of solemnizing such marriage, shall be fined not less than $100 and not more than $1,000 and at the discretion of the Court may also be imprisoned in the County Jail or sentenced to hard labor for not more than six months.

Code, 1907. Section 6221. (Law as to adultery or fornication between two persons not of different race.) A man and woman living together in adultery or fornication for the first conviction, a penalty of a fine of not less than $100, and they may also be imprisoned in the county jail for not more than six months. Second offense with the same person, the penalty a fine of not less than $300, and they may be imprisoned in the county jail, or at hard labor for not more than twelve months. For the third or any subsequent conviction with the same person they must be imprisoned in the penitentiary for two years.

Political Code, 1907, p. 218. Section 2. The term "negro" within the meaning of this Code, includes "mulatto." The term "mulatto" or "person of color" includes persons of mixed blood descended on the part of the father or mother from negro ancestors, to the fifth generation inclusive, though one ancestor of each generation may have been a white person.

The fifth generation was substituted for the third generation by the Code Committee of the 1907 Code. (Prior to this the third generation was the term used in the laws.)

Criminal Code, 1907. Section 7684. Civil Code, 1907. Section 5488. Omits section 4 of Laws 1891, p. 412, containing the penalty for railroads and for conductors and officials neglecting to comply with the law.

1911

General Acts, 1911, p. 677. A Reform School for juvenile negroes shall be established, at Mt. Meiggs, with name "Alabama Reform School for Juvenile Negro Law-Breakers." The school shall have nine trustees, of whom five may be negro women. The school shall be for boys under eighteen years of age, and shall provide a common school education, also training in agriculture and industries, and moral training.

1915

General Acts, 1915, p. 284. Separate lists of white and negro children shall be kept in making school census.

General Acts, 1915, p. 727. Section 1. It is unlawful to require any white female nurse to nurse in wards or rooms in hospitals, either public or private, in which negro men are placed.

Section 2. It is unlawful for any white female nurse to nurse in wards or rooms in hospitals, either public or private, in which negro men are placed.

Section 3. Penalty, a fine of $10 to $200, and there may also be added confinement in county jail, or hard labor for county not exceeding six months.

Alaska

1905

33 Stat. L., p. 619. Schools shall be devoted to the education of white children and children of mixed blood who lead a civilized life.

(Nothing shows whether Indians only, or also negroes, were meant to be included. The wording includes negroes also. Under this wording a mulatto could attend the schools, but a pure negro might apparently be shut out; which was no doubt not the intention of the statute.)

1907

Code, 1907, Part V. Section 199. There shall be no discrimination against negroes in voting requirements.

Arizona

1865

Laws, 1865, p. 58. Marriages of white persons with negroes, mulattoes, Indians, Mongolians, shall be illegal and void. (The word "descendants" is not in this law.)

1901

Revised Statutes. Section 2227. All children between six and twenty-one years of age must be admitted to the public schools.

Section 2231. No child shall be refused admission to any public school on account of race or color. (Original law.)

Revised Statutes, 1901. Section 3092. All marriages of persons of Caucasian blood, or their descendants, with negroes, Mongolians, or Indians, or their descendants, shall be null and void.

Section 3094. Such marriages shall be valid if valid by the laws of the place where contracted, except that residents cannot evade marriage law of this State by going into another State for the ceremony.

1909

Laws, 1909, p. 171, 172. The Trustees of school districts may segregate African pupils from white, when they deem it advisable, and may provide the necessary accommodations for such separation, but only when there are more than eight negro pupils in the school district.

Law passed by the legislature over a veto by the governor.

Arkansas

1866

Laws, 1866, p. 98. Section 1. All colored persons shall have the right to make and enforce contracts, to sue and to be sued, to be affiants, to give evidence, etc., that white persons have. They shall not be subjected to any other or different penalty than provided for white persons. All laws of the state shall be applicable without distinction of color, except as hereinafter provided.

Section 2. Nothing shall be construed to repeal or modify any statute, common law, or usage of the state, respecting marriage of white persons with negroes or mulattoes, voting, service on juries, or militia duties.

Section 3. All negroes cohabiting as husband and wife and recognizing each other as such, shall be deemed lawfully married.

Section 4. All marriages between negroes shall be governed by the same laws as for whites.

Section 5. No negro or mulatto shall be admitted to attend any public school except one exclusively for colored persons.

1868

Constitution, 1868, Article VIII. Section 2. Removed the limitation of the suffrage to whites.

1873

Laws, 1873, p. 15–19. Civil Rights. Section 1. It shall be unlawful for any railway, steamboat, stage-coach, or any other conveyance, to refuse to provide any person with same accommodations as are furnished other persons upon tender of same sum of money actually paid for similar accommodations by any other person.

Section 2. The violation is a misdemeanor punishable by a fine of from $200 to $1,000 or imprisonment of from three months to twelve months, or both.

Section 3. It shall be unlawful for a manager of any public house of entertainment, inn, hotel or restaurant, to refuse to furnish the same meal, board, lodging, room or other accommodation as furnished other persons upon tender of same price actually paid by others.

Section 4. Penalty; a misdemeanor with a fine of from $50 to $500.

Section 5. It is unlawful for any keeper of a licensed saloon, grocery, dram shop, or other place where liquors are sold by retail, to refuse to sell to any person on account of race or color, a drink in the same manner, at the same place, and of the same quality as that sold to others for the same price.

Section 6. Penalty; a misdemeanor with a fine of from $25 to $100.

Section 7. It is unlawful for any manager of a licensed place of public amusement to refuse to admit any person on account of race or color applying to be admitted to a full and free enjoyment of the same, or to refuse to provide the same accommodations given to others for the same payment.

Section 8. Penalty; a misdemeanor with a fine of from $25 to $100.

Section 9. It is unlawful for any school officer of a school, supported in whole or in part by general taxation, to refuse to provide equal and like accommodations and advantages for the education of each and every youth of school age.

Section 10. Penalty; a misdemeanor with a fine of from $100 to $500.

Section 11. Aiding or abetting the violation of any of the provisions of the act is a misdemeanor. Penalty, a fine of from $50 to $500.

Section 12. No person carrying on any business mentioned before, nor any school officer, shall make any rule for the government or conduct of such business, school or institutions, affecting persons applying for accommodation, which shall not affect all alike without regard to race or color.

Section 13. Penalty; in addition to the penalties of preceding sections, the person shall be liable for civil action for damages by the person aggrieved.

Section 14. Prosecuting attorneys, sheriffs, coroners, justices of the peace and constables of this State are authorized and required to institute proceedings on behalf of State, when cognizant of a violation of this Act within their jurisdiction.

Section 15. Any of the aforesaid officers, who are personally cognizant of such offense, or to whom complaints shall be made, who fail to prosecute, shall be guilty of a misdemeanor in office and fined $100 to $500, and the costs of prosecution, or in default of payment, imprisoned for six months, or till the fine and costs are paid. (Repealed, 1907.)

Laws, 1873, p. 423. The Board of school directors shall establish separate schools for white and colored children and youths. It is their duty to provide equal school facilities for blacks and whites.

1884

Digest of Statutes, 1884. Section 4593. All marriages of white persons with negroes or mulattoes are declared illegal and void. (1838, Revised Statutes, p. 536.)

1891

Laws, 1891, March 4. Section 7. In precincts where more than 100 votes were cast on the preceding election, where the electors consist of different races, the judges of election shall, when there are persons of both races present and ready to vote, so conduct admittance to the voting place as to permit persons of white and colored races to cast their votes alternately.

Laws, 1891, p. 15. Section 1. On all lines of railway less than twenty-five miles long the passenger coaches may be divided by partition.

The officers of passenger trains and agents at depots have power to and may be required to assign passengers to the proper place or proper waiting room for each race. Any person insisting on going to the place set apart for another race, shall be fined not less than $10 or more than $200. Any officer of any company wrongly assigning a passenger to such place shall be fined $25. The railway company may refuse to carry passengers who refuse to occupy the place to which they are assigned. The railway company shall have power to eject such a passenger from such improper place and shall not be liable for damages.

Any railway company not complying with the provisions of this act shall be guilty of a misdemeanor and shall be fined not less than $100 nor more than $500 and each day and each train shall be a separate offense. Any conductor, agent or other railway officer not carrying out the provisions of this act shall be fined not less than $25 and not more than $50 for each offense. Railways, other than street railways, shall keep this law posted in a conspicuous place in each passenger coach and waiting room. An exception to the provisions of this act is allowed in the case of an officer with prisoners who may be assigned to the coach set aside for the prisoners' race. A person with visible and distinct admixture of African blood shall be deemed for the purposes of this act to belong to the African race, all others to the white race.

1893

Acts, 1893, p. 200. All railway companies shall provide equal but separate accommodations for the white and colored races, by providing two or more passenger cars for each train, or one car with a partition of wood. There shall also be provided separate waiting rooms equal and sufficient in accommodation at all passenger depots in the State.

The foregoing provisions do not apply to street railways. If the passenger coach is disabled in the event of accident, the railway company shall be relieved from the operation of this act.

No person shall occupy the seats in a coach or apartment or waiting room set apart for members of another race. An exception to this provision shall be made for officers in charge of prisoners of a different race, who may be assigned with their prisoners to coaches where they will least interfere with the comfort of other passengers. The provisions of the act shall not apply to employees of trains in discharge of their duties, nor to freight trains carrying passengers.

Railway companies may haul sleeping or chair cars for the exclusive use of either the white or the African race separately, but not jointly. On all lines of railway less than thirty miles long, passenger coaches may be divided by a partition.

1895

Acts, 1895, April 19. Assessors, county clerks, and collectors, shall indicate on tax list whether a person assessed is of white or colored race. The collector shall indicate the amount of taxes paid respectively by persons of the white and of the colored race.

1897

Acts, 1897, p. 70. The state superintendent of public instruction is authorized to arrange for county normal institutes for white teachers, and such additional ones for the colored teachers at such places as may be selected by the superintendent.

1903

Acts, 1903, p. 178. All persons operating any street-car line in any city of the first class, are required to operate separate cars, or to separate white and colored passengers in cars for both, and to set apart in such car so operated for both, a portion to be occupied by white persons and a portion to be occupied by colored passengers.

No discrimination in quality or convenience of accommodations for the two races shall be made.

The conductor shall have the right to change designation, to decrease or increase space for either race, or may require any passenger to change his seat.

All passengers are required to take the seats assigned. If they refuse they are guilty of a misdemeanor, the fine not to exceed $25.

Any corporation failing to make such separation is guilty of a misdemeanor, the fine not to exceed $25.

Nothing shall prevent running extra or special cars exclusively for either white or colored passengers, if regular cars are operated.

Acts, 1903, p. 161. In the state penitentiary and in all county jails, stockades, convict camps, and all other places where state or county prisoners may at any time be kept confined, separate apartments shall be provided for white and negro prisoners, including separate bunks, beds, bedding, separate dining-tables and all other furnishings. Any such place, or such furnishing, after having been assigned, or used, by one race, it is unlawful to change to the use of the other.

It is unlawful for a white prisoner to be handcuffed or chained or tied to a negro prisoner.

Any prison officer violating the provisions of this act is guilty of a misdemeanor; the fine to be $50 to $200.

1904

Kirby's Digest, 1904. Section 5174. All marriages of white persons with negroes or mulattoes are illegal and void.

Section 2640. The issue of all marriages deemed null in law shall be deemed legitimate.

Kirby's Digest, 1904. Sections 7536 and 7613. The separate school provisions repeated.

1907

Laws, 1907, p. 728. That Chapter 19 of Kirby's Digest known as the "Civil Rights Bill" be, and the same is hereby repealed. (This repealed the Civil Rights Act of 1873 Laws, p. 15.)

California

1849

Constitution, 1849, II. Section 2. Voting limited to white men.

1850

Laws, 1850, p. 424. Section 1. All marriages of white persons with negroes or mulattoes are illegal and void. Contracting such marriage is punishable by a fine of from $100 to $1,000, imprisonment from three months to ten years, or both. (See Civil Code, 1871, par. 60.)

Sections 2, 3. Any person knowingly solemnizing any marriage forbidden by law shall be fined not less than $100 nor more than $1,000, or imprisoned not less than three months nor more than one year, or both.

1854

Laws, 1854, Chapter 54. Section 42. Negroes are forbidden to be witnesses in any case where a white person is a party.

1869–1870

Laws of 1869–1870, p. 838–839. African and Indian children must attend separate schools. Upon written application of the parents or guardians of at least ten such children a separate school shall be established. A less number may be provided for in separate schools in any other manner.

1880

Laws, 1880, p. 38. Children of any race or nationality, from six years to twenty-one years of age inclusive, residing in the district, shall be entitled to admission to the public schools. (Provision repealed the separate school law of 1869–1870.)

1893

Laws, 1893, p. 220. (Civil Rights Law.) It is unlawful to refuse admission to anyone over twenty-one years of age with a ticket of admission acquired by purchase, or with the price of admission, to an opera house, theater, melodeon, museum, circus, caravan, racecourse, fair, or any place of public amusement or entertainment, except that persons of bad character, etc., may be refused. The injured person may recover actual damages and $100 in addition.

1897

Laws, 1897, p. 137. (*Civil Rights law.*) In the usual form, this law specially refers to "Inns, restaurants, hotels, eating houses, barber shops, bath-houses, theaters, skating rinks, and all other places of public accommodation or amusement."

Violating the act or inciting or aiding its violation, rendered the offender liable in damages to not less than $50, recoverable in an action at law. (Civil Code, 1906, p. 29–30.)

1901

Statutes and Amendments, 1900–1901, p. 335. The marriage law was amended, by adding "Mongolian."

Statutes and Amendments, 1900–1901, p. 334. Civil rights law of 1897, p. 137, repeated in somewhat different wording, without real change, except that it omits "hotels" in the section concerning penalty, retaining it elsewhere.

1905

Statutes and Amendments, 1905, p. 553. This statute re-enacted the civil rights law, with word "hotel" again inserted in penalty section.

Colorado

1861

Ter. Laws, 1861, p. 25. Section 5. Voting restricted to free white men.

1864

General Laws, 1864, p. 108. (*Original Law.*) Marriage between negroes and mulattoes, and white persons, is absolutely void. It shall be punished by a fine of not less than $50 and not more than $500, or confinement in prison for not less than three months nor more than two years, or both. (R. S. 1908, Section 4163, 5.)

1876

Constitution, 1876, Article IX. Section 8. Nor shall any distinction or classification of pupils in public schools be made on account of race or color.

1885

Laws, 1885, p. 70. Section 17. In the census alphabetical list, the color shall be given.

Laws, 1885, p. 132. (Civil Rights Act.) All persons regardless of race, color or previous condition of servitude are entitled to the full and equal enjoyment of the accommodations of inns, restaurants, churches, barber shops, public conveyances, theaters, and other places of public resort or amusement.

Violation of the foregoing provisions shall be punished by a fine of not more than $500, or confinement in the county jail not exceeding three months, or both.

1895

Laws, 1895, p. 139. (Civil Rights Act.) All persons are entitled to the full enjoyment of the accommodations and privileges of inns, restaurants, eating houses, barber shops, public conveyances on land or water, theaters and all other places of public accommodation and amusement, subject only to conditions applicable alike to all citizens.

In case of violation of the foregoing provisions, except for reasons applicable alike to citizens of every race and color, and regardless of color or race, there shall be paid by the person so violating a forfeit of a sum not less than $50 and not more than $500 to the person aggrieved. Such violation shall also be a misdemeanor and subject to the penalty of a fine of not less than $10 and not more than $300, imprisonment for not more than one year, or both. Judgment for one shall bar the other prosecution.

1897

Laws, 1897, p. 115. No person shall be denied the right to practise law on account of race or sex.

1907

Laws, 1907, p. 241. Section 7. Certificates of death shall give the race or color.

Laws, 1907, p. 244. Section 14. Birth certificates shall give the color or race of the parents.

1908

Revised Statutes, 1908. Sections 4163, 4165. Marriage between negroes and mulattoes, and white persons, is prohibited. Such a marriage is absolutely void and is a misdemeanor punishable by imprisonment from three months to two years, or a fine of from $50 to $500, or both. Issuing such a license is a misdemeanor, punishable by a fine of $100. Performing the ceremony is punishable by a fine of $50 to $500, or three months to two years' imprisonment, or both.

Connecticut

1833

Laws, 1833, Title 35. No person shall establish in this state any school for the instruction of colored persons not inhabitants of this state, without the consent in writing of the civil authority. A penalty is imposed of a $100 fine for the first offense, and double for every other offense. Nothing in the act shall refer to any district school established under the laws of the state.

1838

Laws, 1838, Title 34. Repealed the preceding law.

1845

Amendments, Article 8, Adopted October, 1845. Every *white* male citizen of the United States is an elector.

1854

General Statutes, 1854, p. 838. Exempted from taxation the personal and real estate of persons of color.

1866

General Statutes, 1866, p. 707. Same as 1854 law. Exempted from taxation personal and real property of persons of color.

1875

General Statutes, 1875, p. 154. Provision stricken out, regarding exemption from taxation, of 1854 and 1866.

1876

Amendments, Article 23, Adopted October, 1876. Article 8 of Amendments to the Constitution is amended by erasing the word "white" from the first line.

1879

Public Acts, 1879, p. 377, Chapter 31. The commander-in-chief is authorized to organize four independent companies of infantry to be composed of colored men. Any existing company of the Wilkins battalion may be accepted as one such company when recruited to the minimum number. Such four companies shall not be attached to any existing regiment unless in case of war, rebellion or invasion, but may be organized into an independent battalion, at discretion of Adjutant-General. The Quartermaster General's duty is to provide such companies with armories, arms, and equipment, from any supplies he may have, upon the same terms and conditions as other companies of infantry are now provided, also with uniforms of the same quality as for other companies. Said four companies shall receive the same pay and allowances as other companies for one company parade in the Spring and one in the month of September in each year, also the same pay and allowances when ordered into service or ordered into encampment.

1883

Laws, 1883, Chapter 109, p. 289. Section 15. Negro Militia. Chapter 31 of the Public Acts of 1879 and all acts and parts of acts inconsistent herewith are hereby repealed, but this act shall not affect the organization heretofore and now existing under the provisions of said Chapter 31, but the companies comprising the same shall belong to the battalion at large as herein provided. The forty companies of infantry shall be organized into four regiments, one for each congressional district—and one battalion at large. The battalion at large shall consist of not more than four companies and shall be commanded by a major.

1884

Laws, 1884, p. 366. (*Offences v. the person.*) Every person who subjects or causes to be subjected any other person to the deprivation of any rights, privileges or immunities secured or protected by the Constitution or Laws of this State, or of the United States, on account of alienage, color, or race, shall be fined not more than $1,000, or imprisoned not more than one year, or both.

1887

Laws, 1887, p. 690. Section 1. (*Life Insurance.*) No Life Insurance Company shall make any distinction or discrimination between white persons and colored persons, wholly or partially of African descent, as to the premiums or rates charged for policies upon the lives of such persons, nor demand greater premiums from such colored persons, nor make any rebate, diminution or discount upon the sum to be paid in case of death of such colored person insured, nor insert in policy any condition nor make any stipulation whereby such person shall bind himself to accept any sum less than full value on account of such policy other than imposed upon white persons in similar cases, and every such stipulation or condition so made or inserted shall be void.

Section 2. (*Affidavit of Examining Physician.*) If an application of a colored person for insurance upon his life is refused, the company shall furnish an affidavit of a regular examining physician of such company who has made the examination stating that the application has been refused, not because of color but solely on such grounds as would be applicable to white persons of the same age and sex.

Section 3. (*Penalty for discrimination in issuing policies.*) Every corporation, or officer or agent, violating the preceding sections by demanding or receiving from colored persons any different or greater premium, or allowing discount or rebate on premiums paid or to be paid by white persons of the same age and sex, general condition of health and hope of longevity, or by making rebate or diminution upon sum to be paid upon policy in case of death, or by failing to furnish affidavit required by previous section, shall be fined not more than $100 (but this shall not affect contracts existing June 1, 1887).

1889

Laws, 1889, p. 74. (*Discrimination in favor of individuals prohibited.*) No Life Insurance Company shall make distinction or discrimination in favor of individuals between insurants of same class and expectation of life in amount of premiums or dividends or benefits, or in any other of the terms or conditions, nor shall any company, agent, broker or any other person, make any contract of insurance or agreement other than is plainly expressed in the policy issued thereon; nor shall any company or agent pay, allow or offer as inducement to insurance any rebate of premium or any special favor or any inducement whatever not specified in the policy of insurance.

1905

Public Acts, 1905, p. 323, Chapter III. Every person who deprives or causes to be deprived another of the full and equal enjoyment of the advantages, facilities, accommodations or privileges of any place of public accommodation, amusement or transportation, on account of alienage, race or color, or who on that account shall discriminate in the price for the enjoyment of such privileges, subject only to the limitations established by law for all persons, shall forfeit to the person injured thereby double damages.

Delaware

1867

Laws, 1866–1869, p. 161. The punishment for members of all races shall be the same, for the same offense.

1873

Laws, 1871–1873, p. 686. Resolved; That the members of this General Assembly, for the people they represent, and for themselves, jointly and individually, do hereby declare uncompromising opposition to a proposed act of Congress, introduced by Honorable Charles Sumner at the last session, and now on file in the Senate of the United States, known as the "Supplemental Civil Rights Bill," and all other measures intended or calculated to equalize or amalgamate the negro race with the white race, politically or socially, and especially do they proclaim unceasing opposition to making negroes eligible to public offices, to sit on juries, and to their admission into public schools where white children attend, and to the admission on terms of equality with white people in the churches, public conveyances, places of amusement, or hotels, and to any measure designed or having the effect to promote the equality of the negro with the white man in any of the relations of life, or which may possibly conduce to such result.

That our Senators in Congress be instructed, and our Representatives requested, to vote against and use all honorable means to defeat the passage by Congress of the bill referred to in the foregoing resolution, known as the "Supplemental Civil Rights Bill," and all other measures of a kindred nature, and any and every attempt to make the negro the peer of the white man.

1874

Revised Statutes, 1874, p. 207. The schools shall be free to all the white children of a district. (Revised Statutes, 1852, p. 115.)

Revised Statutes, 1874, p. 472. Marriage is unlawful between white persons and negroes. A fine of $100 is imposed upon the parties to such a marriage, and upon the preacher solemnizing it. (Revised Statutes, 1829, p. 400.)

Revised Statutes, 1874, p. 485. A negro or mulatto child under fifteen, whom parents cannot maintain—or do not bring up to industry and suitable employment—may be bound as a servant till twenty-one years of age if a male, or eighteen years of age if a female. (White persons were bound as apprentices, not servants.)

If he [such servant] run away or absent himself without leave he shall make full compensation for lost time and the expenses of recovering him. The Superior Court shall have power so to extend the term.

If such female servant have a bastard child, she shall serve one year after expiration of the original term.

If such servant marry without written consent, he shall be given six months' extended term.

Idle and vagabond free negroes and free mulattoes may be compulsorily hired out to service. The constable may be ordered to hire out said negro or mulatto as a servant, at public auction for the residue of the current year.

1875

Laws, 1875–1877, Volume 15, p. 322. No keeper of an inn, tavern, hotel or restaurant, or other place of public entertainment or refreshment of travellers, guests, or customers, shall be obliged by law to furnish entertainment or refreshment to persons whose reception or entertainment by him would be offensive to the major part of his customers and would injure his business. The term customers shall be taken to include all who have occasion for entertainment or refreshment.

Section 2. The proprietor of a theater or other place of public amusement shall not be obliged to receive into his show or admit into the place where he is pursuing his occupation any persons whose reception or entertainment by him would be offensive to the major part of his customers and would injure his business.

Section 3. Carriers of passengers may assign a particular place in their cars, carriages or boats, to such of their customers as they may choose to place there, and whose presence elsewhere would be offensive to the major part of the travelling public, where their business is conducted. The quality of accommodation shall be equal for all, if the same price for carriage is required from all.

1877

Laws, 1877, p. 82. Imposed a separate tax on colored people for the benefit of colored schools. A separate fund was created, to be used by the Delaware association for the education of colored people.

1883

Laws, 1883, p. 81. Money collected from the colored people's school tax must be used for the education of colored children. The State Superintendent of Schools was given charge.

1889

Laws, 1889, p. 147. Act to encourage education of the colored people. Taxes property of colored persons for support of colored schools.

Section 2. A separate fund for colored schools is provided.

Section 3. $6,000 was appropriated annually.

Section 4. The superintendents of Free Schools were given control of the schools.

Laws, 1889, pp. 651, 655, 658, 660, 663. Incorporated colored schools were established, under boards of trustees elected by the school district.

1891

Laws, 1891, Chapter 66. Section 7. Free text-books for colored schools shall be furnished.

Section 10. County superintendents shall have entire management and control of the colored schools of the state.

Laws, 1891, Chapter 119, p. 354. A State College for Colored Students is provided, to instruct in agriculture, mechanical arts, English language, etc., with special reference to application to industries of life. Other scientific and classical studies may be taught, and a normal school may be connected.

1893

Code, 1893, p. 593. Section 1. Repeats intermarriage law of 1852. (Revised Statutes, 1852, p. 236.)

Section 2. Negroes or mulattoes may be married without license or banns, provided they produce a certificate of a justice of the peace that they have made satisfactory proof of freedom; or being a servant—shall produce written consent of master. Performing ceremony without this—$20 fine. A free person marrying with a servant without consent must pay to master $30 if man and $15 if woman.

Laws, 1893, p. 693. Section 14. Incorporated colored schools are abolished, and they shall be subject to the same laws and under the supervision of the superintendent of schools for the county, in the same manner as is now provided for unincorporated colored schools.

Section 15. Money appropriated for the support of colored schools shall be paid direct to the superintendents of schools to be by them expended for the support of the colored schools.

Laws, 1893, Chapter 638. Any colored boy, under the age of twelve —who is an orphan or abandoned by his parents and uncared for— may be committed to "St. Joseph's Society for Colored Missions of Wilmington," during the term of his minority.

1895

Laws, 1895, p. 19. Various provisions to improve and promote colored schools. No change in privileges or restrictions.

1897

Laws, 1897, p. 431. Various provisions for colored schools. No change in privileges or restructions.

Laws, 1897, p. 433. Delaware Colored Teachers State Institute is established.

1898

Laws, 1898, p. 193. Schools in districts for white schools shall be free for all white children of the district of six years of age and over, and similar provision is made for colored schools. It is provided that any district may establish a kindergarten, which shall or may be free for all the white or colored children (as the case may be), of the age of four years or over.

1911

Laws, 1911, p. 682. Marriage is unlawful between a white person and a negro or mulatto.

Such marriage is void. It is a misdemeanor, punishable by a fine of $100, or in default of payment, confinement in prison not exceeding thirty days is inflicted.

Issuing a license, or solemnizing the marriage knowingly, is a misdemeanor, punishable by a fine of $100, or in default of payment, imprisonment not exceeding thirty days.

If the marriage was solemnized outside of the state, after which the parties live and cohabit within the state as husband and wife, it is a misdemeanor, with same penalty as if the marriage had occurred in the state.

1913

Laws, 1913, p. 259. A hospital for colored consumptives is authorized, under the care of the Delaware State Tuberculosis Commission.

Florida

1865

Laws, 1865, p. 24. It is a capital crime to assault a white female with intent to commit rape, or to be accessory thereto.

Laws, 1865, p. 24. If any negro, mulatto, or other person of color shall intrude himself into any railroad car or other public vehicle set apart for the exclusive accommodation of white people, he shall be deemed guilty of a misdemeanor and, upon conviction, shall be sentenced to stand in the pillory for one hour, or be whipped, not exceeding thirty-nine stripes, or both, at the discretion of the jury, nor shall it be lawful for any white person to intrude himself into any railroad car or other public vehicle set apart for the exclusive accommodation of persons of color, under the same penalties.

Laws, 1865, p. 30. A person of color is one who has as much as one-eight negro blood.

Constitution, 1865, XIV. Section 2. Negroes are permitted to testify only in proceedings founded upon injury to a negro, or in cases affecting the rights and remedies of negroes.

Laws, 1865, pp. 35–36. A statute relative to testimony in general. It provided that the testimony of negroes should not be taken by deposition in writing or upon written interrogation, or "otherwise than in such manner as will enable the court or jury to judge the credibility of the witness."

1866

Laws, 1865, p. 31. Remarriage. All colored persons living together as husband and wife, who are not legally married, who wish to continue living together, are required to be married within nine months from the date of the passage of the act. If they fail to be married, and continue to live together, punished as guilty of fornication and adultery. Their children legitimated by the marriage.

After nine months from passage of act, all laws as to marriage between white persons shall apply to colored population.

Laws, 1866, p. 22. (*Statute amended.*) If persons of color live together as husband and wife and recognize each other as such, they are considered married, and their children legitimate.

1868

Constitution, 1868, XIV. Section 1. Granted suffrage to negroes, removing the limitation to white persons.

1873

Laws, 1873, p. 25, Chapter 1947. (*Civil Rights Bill.*) Prohibition of discrimination on account of race, color, or previous condition of servitude, in the full and equal enjoyment of the accommodations, etc., of inns, public conveyances on land and water, licensed theaters, other places of public amusement, common schools, public institutions of learning, cemeteries, and benevolent associations supported by general taxation. The prohibition does not apply to private schools or cemeteries established exclusively for white or for colored persons. Discrimination in any laws by the use of the word "white," is prohibited.

1881

Digest Laws, 1881, p. 753. Section 8. It is not lawful for any white person to intermarry with any negro person. Such marriage is null and void and the issue bastard.

Issuing the license or performing the ceremony is punishable by a fine of $1,000 of which one-half shall be paid to the informer. (Laws, 1832, January 23.)

1885

Constitution, 1885, Article XII. Section 12. White and colored children shall not be taught in the same school, but impartial provision shall be made for both.

Constitution, 1885, Article XVI. Section 24. All marriages between a white person and a negro, or between a white person and a person of negro descent to the fourth generation inclusive, are hereby forever prohibited.

1887

Acts, 1887, p. 116. Sections 1 and 2. Railroad companies shall sell to all respectable negro persons first-class tickets at the same rates as to white persons and shall furnish and set apart for negro persons a car in each train equally as good and provided with the same facilities for comfort as for white persons. No white person shall be permitted to ride in a negro car or to insult or annoy any negro in such car. No negro shall ride in a white person's car; but female colored nurses having care of children or of sick persons may ride in the white person's car.

Section 3. Any conductor or railroad company violating the provisions of this act as to accommodations of white and colored persons, is liable to a fine not exceeding $500.

Section 4. In case of a railroad company not complying with this act, punishment may be inflicted upon the president, receiver, general manager, or superintendent thereof, or upon each and every one of them.

Constitution, 1887, Article XII. Section 12. White and colored children shall not be taught in the same school, but impartial provision shall be made for both.

1892

Acts, 1892, p. 269. A colored normal school established at Tallahassee.

1895

Acts, 1895, p. 96. It shall be a penal offense for any individual or association to conduct any school, on any grade, either public or private, wherein white persons and negroes are instructed or boarded in the same building, or are taught in the same class, or at the same time by the same teachers.

The violation of this act by either patronizing or teaching in such a school shall be punished by a fine not less than $150 and not more than $500, or by imprisonment in the county jail for not less than three months and not more than six months. (General Statutes, 1906, Section 3810.)

1897

Acts, 1897, Chapter 4165. Section 3. Florida Industrial School for Boys. (Reform School.) It shall have two separate buildings, not nearer than one-quarter mile, one for white and one for negro boys. White and negro convicts shall not in any manner be associated together or worked together.

1899

Acts, 1899, Chapter 4749, p. 135. Section 1. Where persons of African blood have prior to January 1, 1866, cohabited and lived together as husband and wife, and prior to said date, recognized each other before world and were recognized as husband and wife, they are deemed such so long as such relationship existed between them, and their children are legitimate.

1903

Acts, 1903, Chapter 5, 140, p. 76. Section 1. Intermarriage with a negro, mulatto, or any person with one-eighth negro blood shall be punished by imprisonment not exceeding ten years or fine not exceeding $1,000. Such marriage is utterly null and void.

A county judge knowingly issuing a license shall be punished by imprisonment not exceeding two years, or a fine not exceeding $1,000.

Performing such a ceremony shall be punished by imprisonment not exceeding one year, or a fine not exceeding $1,000.

The living in adultery or fornication of a white person and a negro or mulatto, shall be punished by imprisonment not exceeding twelve months or a fine not exceeding $1,000.

Any negro man and white woman (or the reverse), not married to each other, who shall habitually live in and occupy in the night time the same room, no other person over fifteen years of age being present, shall each be punished by imprisonment not exceeding twelve months or a fine not exceeding $500. (See General Statutes, 1906, Section 3529, etc.)

Acts, 1903, Chapter 5202. Section 22. In no case shall any colored officer command white troops.

1905

Acts, 1905, Chapter 5447. Section 1. It shall be unlawful for any officer to chain white female or male prisoners to colored prisoners in their charge. Violation shall be a misdemeanor, punishable by a fine not exceeding $100, or confinement in the county jail not exceeding six months, or both.

Acts, 1905, p. 99. Separation of races is required on all street railways. The company must provide either separate cars, or divisions within the car. Exception is made of colored nurses in attendance upon white children or white sick persons. Failure to enforce such separation on part of company shall be punished by a fine of $50 for each offense. A passenger occupying wrong division shall be punished by fine of $25 or by imprisonment of twenty days.

39 Southern, 398, at p. 400. (50 Florida, 127.) The court declared the above exception (in Laws, 1905, p. 99) contrary to the Fourteenth Amendment, as giving a Caucasian mistress right to have her child attended in the Caucasian department of the car by its African nurse, and withholding from an African mistress the equal right to have her child attended in the African department by its Caucasian nurse.

1907

Acts, 1907, Chapter 5617. Section 1. Urban and suburban (or either) electric cars as common carriers of passengers shall furnish equal but separate accommodations for white and negro passengers.

Section 2. Separate cars, fixed divisions, movable screens, or other methods of division in cars, shall be provided.

Section 3. Urban and suburban electric cars. The failure to provide such separation is a misdemeanor, punishable by a fine of from $50 to $500, which may be enforced against the president, receiver, general manager, superintendent, or other person operating such cars.

Section 4. Each day of such refusal, failure, or neglect is a separate and distinct offense.

Section 5. Any conductor, etc., failing to enforce such separation is guilty of a misdemeanor, punishable by a fine not exceeding $25, or by imprisonment in the county jail not exceeding sixty days, or both.

Section 6. Any passenger wilfully occupying the place of other race, is guilty of a misdemeanor, punishable by a fine not exceeding $50, or by imprisonment in the county jail not exceeding three months, or both. The conductor is vested with full power and authority to arrest such a passenger and to eject him from the car.

Section 7. Plain letters in conspicuous place, "For White," "For Colored."

Section 8. Nothing in this act shall be so construed as to apply to nurses of one race attending children or invalids of the other race.

Section 9. This shall not prevent running of special or extra cars, in addition to regular schedule cars, for the exclusive accommodation of either white or negro passengers.

Acts, 1907, Chapter 5619. Section 1. Separate waiting rooms and ticket windows must be provided for white and colored persons at all depots.

Section 2. The railroad commissioners of the State of Florida are authorized to require the building or the alteration of all depots so as to secure separation of white and colored passengers.

Section 3. Any railroad company refusing to comply with the provisions of act or the regulations of the railroad commissioners, are liable to a fine not exceeding $5,000, to be imposed by the railroad commissioners.

1909

Acts, 1909, p. 171. The county commissioners of the respective counties are required, within twelve months from the passage of this act, so to arrange the jails that it shall be unnecessary to confine in the same room, cell, or apartment, white and negro prisoners, or male or female prisoners. As soon as the jails are so arranged that this section may be complied with, it shall be unlawful for white and negro, or male and female, prisoners to be confined in the county jails in same cell, room or apartment, or so confined as to be permitted to commingle together. The county commissioners are authorized to appropriate from the general revenue fund of the county such money as is necessary. Any board of county commissioners and any sheriff wilfully refusing to comply with the provisions of this act shall be removed from office by the Governor.

Acts, 1909, Chapter 5893. Section 1. Separate accommodations required. Passengers on railroads are required to occupy the respective cars or divisions of cars for their race. No railroad shall use divided cars for separate races without the permission of the railroad commission, nor any car in which the divisions are not permanent.

Section 2. The railroad commissioners of the State of Florida are given power and authority to prescribe reasonable rules and regulations relating to the separation of white and colored passengers in passenger cars operated by any common carrier.

Section 3. If any common carrier violate any of the provisions of this act, or any regulation of the railroad commissioners, a fine not exceeding $500 may be imposed by the railroad commissioners.

Section 4. A passenger occupying a place set apart for the other race, may be fined not exceeding $500 or confined not exceeding six months. An exception is made of persons lawfully in charge of or under charge of persons of other race.

1913

Acts, 1913, p. 311. From the time of the passage of this act, it shall be unlawful in this state, for white teachers to teach negroes in negro schools, and for negro teachers to teach in white schools. Violation shall be punished by a fine not to exceed $500, or by imprisonment in county jail not to exceed six months.

Georgia

1865–1866

Acts, 1865–1866, p. 239. All negroes, mulattoes, mestizos, and their descendants, having one-eighth negro or African blood, shall be known as persons of color.

Acts, 1865–1866, p. 239. Colored persons living together on March 9, 1866, as husband and wife, shall be regarded as such. If any man or woman lived with more than one husband or wife, he shall choose one of them, and the ceremony of marriage shall be performed between these two. If he fail to choose, he or she shall be guilty of fornication or adultery.

Every colored child born before March 9, 1866, is a legitimate child of his mother, but only a legitimate child of his colored father when born within what was regarded as wedlock.

Acts, 1865–1866, p. 241. Any officer issuing a marriage license to parties, either of whom is of African descent and the other a white person, shall be guilty of a misdemeanor and fined not less than $200 nor more than $500, or confined in the common jail three months, or both.

Any officer, or minister of the Gospel, marrying such persons together, shall be guilty of a misdemeanor, and fined not less than $500 nor more than $1,000, or confined in the common jail for six months, or both. (See Code, 1861, Section 1664.) (Nothing as to intermarriage appears to be contained in the codes of 1821, 1837, or 1859. But see Acts, 1859, p. 54.)

1865

Constitution, 1865, Article II. Section 5, Paragraph 4. It shall be the duty of the General Assembly to prescribe when testimony of negroes shall be admitted in courts.

Constitution, 1865, Article II. Section 5. Paragraph 5. The General Assembly at its next session shall pass a law legalizing existing slave marriages, and arranging for future marriages, and regulating the right of negroes to devise and inherit property.

1866

Acts, 1866, p. 59. Any free white citizen shall be entitled to instruction in schools free of charge.

Acts, 1866, p. 156. Ordained colored ministers may celebrate marriage for persons of African descent only, under same regulations as required for white citizens.

1868

Constitution, 1868, Article II. Section 2. Removed the limitation of the suffrage to whites only.

1870

Acts, 1870, p. 427, 428. Railroads are required to furnish equal accommodations to all, without regard to race, color or previous condition of servitude. Any railroad violating this requirement may be sued and the person wronged recover such sum as the court thinks proper, not to exceed $10,000.

1872

Laws, 1872, p. 69. It shall be the duty of the Board of Education to make arrangements for the instruction of the children of white and negro races in separate schools. As far as practicable they shall provide the same facilities for both races in respect to attainments and abilities of teachers and the length of term time; but the children of the white and colored races shall not be taught together in any public school of this state. Schools admitting both races shall receive none of the public school fund.

1874

Laws, 1874, p. 109. Section 1116. Returns shall be made to the comptroller-general of the state of all taxes paid by colored taxpayers. He shall show these in his annual report.

1877

Constitution, Article 8. Section 1. The schools shall be free to all children of the state, but separate schools shall be provided for the white and colored races.

1885

Laws, 1885, p. 399. Asylums are to have separate apartments for insane negroes.

1891

Laws, 1890–1891, p. 157. All railroads shall furnish equal accommodations, in separate cars or compartments of cars, for white and for colored passengers, but this section shall not apply to sleeping-cars.

Railroad companies shall furnish comfortable seats, and have cars well and sufficiently lighted and ventilated. Violation a misdemeanor.

Conductors must assign passengers to their place; and all conductors of dummy, electric and street cars are required to assign passengers to seats, so as to separate the white and colored races as much as practicable; and all conductors, etc., are invested with police powers to carry out these provisions.

If the passenger remains in the wrong place it is a misdemeanor. The conductor is given right to eject him.

Where the car is divided into compartments, the space shall be proportioned to the usual and ordinary travel.

Employees shall not allow white and colored passengers to occupy the same compartment. Violation by an employee is a misdemeanor.

This does not apply to nurses or servants in attendance upon employers.

Laws, 1890–1891, p. 213. No person controlling convicts shall confine white and colored convicts together, or work them chained together, or chain them going to and from their work or at any other time. Violating this provision by any person or any member of a firm is a misdemeanor.

The Prison Commission, where practicable, shall employ white persons and negroes in separate institutions and locations, and they shall be provided with separate eating and sleeping apartments.

1893

Laws, 1893, p. 121. Inmates of reformatories shall be separated according to color.

1894

Laws, 1894, p. 31. The names of colored and of white tax-payers shall be made out separately on the tax digest.

1895

Code, 1895. Section 1378. Colored and white children shall not attend the same school. No teacher receiving or teaching white and colored pupils in the same school shall be allowed any compensation out of the common school fund.

1897

Laws, 1897, p. 70. Section 679. Upon the penal farm, the commission shall provide for keeping separate and apart the white and colored convicts when not at work, and when at work as far as practicable.

1899

Laws, 1899, p. 66. Sleeping-car companies and railroad companies shall have the right to assign all passengers to seats and berths, and shall separate white and colored passengers in sleeping-cars in making assignments. They shall not permit white and colored passengers to occupy the same compartment.

Passenger remaining in other compartment than assigned is guilty of a misdemeanor.

This act shall not be construed to compel such companies to carry persons of color in sleeping-cars or parlor cars.

The act shall not apply to colored nurses or servants, traveling with employers.

Conductors and employees shall have police powers to enforce the provisions of the act. Refusing or failing to eject a passenger who is violating the provisions of the act, is a misdemeanor.

1905

Laws, 1905, p. 117. Any person may grant to any municipal corporation lands for a park, and in said conveyance provide that the use of said park shall be limited to the white race only, or to white women and children only, or to the colored race, etc., or to any other race, or women and children of any other race only.

Any municipal corporation may accept such a gift for the exclusive use of the class named.

Laws, 1905, p. 166. Abolished colored troops of the state, active and retired, and discharged men and officers from the military service of state.

1912

Laws, 1912, pp. 162, 171. (*Ann. Code, 1914, Section 1525 m.*) The board of education shall provide separate schools for the white and colored races, to extend on an equitable basis the benefits of the law to white and colored children, due regard being had to differences in population.

1914

Annotated Code, 1914. Section 6581. The General Assembly may make appropriations of money to any college or university (not exceeding one in number), now established or hereafter to be established, in this state, for the education of persons of color.

Annotated Code, 1914. Section 1596. Insane negroes shall be separated in a class by themselves, in the Georgia State Sanitarium.

Section 1611. Apartments must be provided for insane negroes.

Idaho

1867

Laws, 1866–1867, p. 71. Section 3. All marriages of white persons with negroes, mulattoes, Indians, or Chinese, are illegal and void.

Section 4. Such marriages, and the solemnizing of them, constitute a misdemeanor, punishable by fine of from $100 to $1,000, or imprisonment from three months to ten years.

1887

Revised Statutes. Section 2425. Intermarriage. Same provision as Laws, 1866–1867, p. 71, Section 3.

1889

Constitution, 1889, Article IX. Section 6. No distinction or classification of pupils in schools shall be made on account of race or color.

1908

Revised Code, 1908, I. Section 2616. Intermarriage is prohibited between negroes and white persons and is illegal and void. A marriage valid where consummated outside this state is valid in Idaho.

Illinois

1819

Laws, 1819, p. 354. Negroes coming into the state to settle must have a certificate of freedom and must register at the clerk's office. Resident negroes also were required to register.

1827

Laws, 1827, February 2. Section 3. A negro or mulatto shall not be a witness in court against a white person. A person with one-quarter part negro blood is a mulatto. (Revised Statutes, 1845, p. 154.)

1848

Constitution, 1848, Article VI. Section 1. Voting is limited to white males.

1853

Public Laws, 1853, p. 57. It is a misdemeanor for a negro to come into the state with intention of residing. Such negroes shall be prosecuted and fined, or sold for a time to pay the fine.

1865

Public Laws, 1865, p. 105. Repealed act making it a misdemeanor for a negro to come into the state to reside.

1874

Laws, 1874, approved, March 24. (1874, Revised Statutes, p. 983.)

Article XVI. Section 4. All boards of education, etc., are prohibited from excluding from the public schools, directly or indirectly, any child on account of the color of such child.

Any school officer, who shall exclude, or aid in excluding from the public schools, on account of color, any child who is entitled to the benefits of such school, shall be fined, upon conviction, not less than $5 nor more than $100.

Any person who shall by threats, menace, or intimidation, prevent any colored child entitled to attend a public school, from attending such school, may be fined not exceeding $25.

1885

Laws, 1885, p. 64. (*Civil Rights Act.*) All persons shall be entitled to the equal privileges of inns, restaurants, eating-houses, barber-shops, public conveyances on land or water, theaters and all other places of public accommodation and amusement, subject only to conditions applicable alike to all citizens.

Any person violating this act by denying the provisions thereof, or of inciting another to such denial, shall forfeit and pay not less than $25 nor more than $500 to the person aggrieved; and shall also be guilty of a misdemeanor, and subject to a fine of not more than $500, or imprisonment not more than one year, or both. Judgment in favor of the party aggrieved or punishment following upon an indictment, shall be a bar to either prosecution respectively.

1891

Laws, 1891, p. 85. The Civil Rights Law of 1885 was amended by adding the following. Justices of the Peace in the county wherein an offense shall be committed shall have jurisdiction in all civil cases, etc.

On appeal, the Appellate Court shall have jurisdiction to render judgment for a sum exceeding the jurisdiction of a Justice of the Peace.

Laws, 1891, p. 163. Marriages where one or both of parties were slaves at the time, are valid, and the children are legitimate, and placed on same footing as to right to inherit property as children of other marriages. Provisions of act extend to such marriages entered into without the state, as far as property within state is concerned.

1896

Statutes, 1896, p. 3730. Section 292. School officers are prohibited from excluding children from the public schools directly or indirectly on account of color. Penalty, $5 to $100 fine.

1897

Laws, 1897, p. 137. Section 1 of the Civil Rights Law of 1885 was amended, adding, hotels, soda-fountains, saloons, bathrooms, theaters, skating-rinks, concerts, cafes, bicycle-rinks, elevators, ice-cream parlors or rooms, railroads, omnibusses, stages, street-cars, boats.

1903

Laws, 1903, p. 158. Civil Rights Law of 1885 extended to include funeral hearses. (The title and enacting clause were irregular.) Section 1 was amended to read as follows. Inns, restaurants, eating houses, hotels, soda-fountains, saloons, barber shops, bath-rooms, theaters, skating-rinks, concerts, cafes, bicycle-rinks, elevators, ice-cream parlors or rooms, railroads, omnibusses, stages, street cars, boats, funeral hearses, public conveyances on land and water, and all other places of public accommodation and amusement, subject only to conditions applicable alike to all citizens.

1911

Laws, 1911, p. 288. Amendment to Civil Rights Law of 1885 as subsequently amended, by adding thereto the following. Nor shall there be any discrimination on account of race or color in the price to be charged and paid for lots or graves in any cemetery or place for burying the dead, but the price shall be applicable alike to all citizens of every race and color.

1915

Laws, 1915, p. 96. Appropriated $25,000 for an exhibition and celebration to commemorate the fiftieth anniversary of the emancipation of the Negro. Created a commission to conduct the same.

Indiana

1843

Revised Statutes, p. 314. Public schools. The law provided for a tax levy for support of schools, but omitted "all negroes and mulattoes" from the tax list. See court interpretation in 1850.

Revised Statutes, 1843, p. 718. Section 251. Evidence of Indians and negroes is prohibited, except where negroes or Indians only are parties.

Revised Statutes, 1843, p. 595. No white person shall marry any negro or mulatto. (1843 Laws, p. 970.) No white person and person of one-eighth or more negro blood shall intermarry. Penalty, hard labor in state prison from one year to ten years, and a fine from $1,000 to $5,000.

1850

2 Indiana, p. 332. (1850.) The court held negro children could not be received in schools even if paying their own tuition, if white parents objected.

Constitution, 1851, Article II. Section 2. Voting was limited to white males.

Constitution, 1851, Article XIII. Prohibits any free negro or mulatto from coming into state; and persons who employ or encourage them to remain in the state are fined $10 to $500. The fines shall go to a fund for the colonization of negroes.

1861

Acts, 1861, p. 153. Lands to be conveyed. No person except a citizen of United States, or an alien at the time a bona fide resident of the United States, an Indian, a Negro, or a Mulatto, or other person of mixed blood—shall convey land except in such cases as are provided for by law.

1862

Revised Statutes, 1862, p. 166. Same as 1843, Revised Statutes, p. 718, on evidence.

Revised Statutes, 1862, p. 429. Intermarriage law of 1843 repeated. (Revised Statutes, 1852, p. 361.)

1863

Laws, 1863. No Colonization Act for Negroes appears in the 1863 statutes, though referred to as follows in Laws, 1865, p.63.

1865

Laws, 1865, p. 63. Whereas the colonization agent appointed (for the colonization of free negroes) is drawing an annual salary without rendering any adequate service to the state, the Act of 1863 for Colonization of Negroes is repealed.

Laws, 165, p. 162. All persons shall be competent as witnesses without distinction as to color or blood, but no negro or mulatto who has come or shall thereafter come into the state contrary to Thirteenth Article of the Constitution prohibiting immigration of free negroes shall be competent as a witness where a white person is a party in interest in a case, while said article continues in force. When the negro excluded is a party in a case, his opponent shall also be excluded.

1866

26 Indiana, 299. (1866.) Preceding statute held against Federal Constitution, on ground that the negro had become a citizen, and as such was entitled to migrate from one state to another.

1867

Laws, 1867, p. 225. Every competent person is allowed to testify.

1869

Laws, 1869, p. 41. School trustees shall organize colored children into separate schools having all the rights and privileges of other schools. If there is not a sufficient number within attending distance, several districts may be consolidated. If there is not a sufficient number thus to be consolidated, the trustees shall provide other means of education for said children or shall use their proportion of school revenue to the best advantage.

1877

Acts, 1877, p. 124. Section 6581. School trustees of any township, town, or city may organize the colored children into separate schools, having all the rights, privileges and advantages of other schools, Provided that in case there may not be provided separate schools for the colored children, then they shall be allowed to attend the public schools with the white children; Provided further that when any child in a colored school shall make sufficient advancement to be in a higher grade than afforded by colored schools, as shown by examination or certificate, he shall be entitled to enter a school for white children of like grade, and no distinction shall therein be made on account of race or color of such colored child.

1879

Laws, 1879, p. 228. Section 4335. Distinction prohibited. In administering the charity of any association (for the care of orphans) no distinction shall be made in selecting the objects of its care on the account of the nativity of such orphans, and associations formed for the purpose of maintaining an asylum for colored orphan children, exclusively, shall be entitled to the allowance provided in this act for each colored orphan child cared for (an allowance of so much per day for any orphan cared for).

1885

Acts, 1885, p. 76. (1908, Burns Annotated Statutes, Section 3863.) All persons shall be entitled to the full enjoyment of the accommodation of inns, restaurants, eating-houses, barber-shops, public conveyances on land and water, theaters, and all places of public accommodation and amusement, subject only to conditions applicable alike to all citizens. Any one violating this act or inciting such violation shall forfeit and pay to the person aggrieved a sum not to exceed $100; also he shall be guilty of a misdemeanor and subject to a fine not to exceed $100 or imprisonment not more than thirty days or both.

No citizen possessing other qualifications shall be disqualified to serve as grand or petit juror in any court on account of race or color. Any officer excluding or failing to summon any citizen for cause aforesaid is guilty of a misdemeanor and shall be fined not more than $100, or imprisoned for not more than thirty days, or both.

1908

Annotated Statutes, 1908. Sections 2641–2642 and 8367. Intermarriage is prohibited between white persons and persons having one-eighth or more negro blood. Counselling or assisting such intermarriage is subject to a fine of from $100 to $1,000. Such intermarriage knowingly, if the white person knows the other is of negro or mixed blood, is subject to fine of not less than $100 nor more than $1,000, or imprisonment in state prison not less than one nor more than ten years. The marriage is void.

1909

Acts, 1909, p. 315. The Adjutant General shall provide for the organization, maintenance and discipline of a battalion of colored infantry of the Indiana National Guard in accordance with the provisions of the law for the organization, maintenance and discipline of the Indiana National Guard.

Iowa

1838–1839

Laws, 1838–1839, p. 65. Certificates of freedom are required of blacks coming to reside in the state, with a bond and security.

1839–1840

Laws, 1839–1840, Chapter 25. Section 13. The marriage of white persons with negroes and mulattoes is illegal and void. (Does not appear in laws again. Omitted in Code of 1851.)

1846

Constitution, 1846, Article II. Section 1. Voting is limited to white males.

Laws, 1846, Chapter 99. Section 66. The schools shall be open and free to all white persons.

1848

Laws, 1848, Chapter 80. Section 51. White persons only are recognized in the school list.

1851

Code, 1851. Section 1160. All property of blacks and mulattoes is exempt from taxation for school purposes.

Laws, 1851, p. 172. Free negroes or mulattoes were not to settle in state. They must be notified to leave by township and county officers in three days. If they did not leave, they were subject to arrest, fine of $2 for each day of staying after notice, and costs. They must be confined in jail till fine was paid and they consented to leave. Free negroes in the state were to remain.

1857

Constitution, 1857, Article I. Section 1. All men have certain inalienable rights such as enjoying and defending life and liberty, acquiring property, and pursuing and obtaining safety and happiness. (Held that this forbids discrimination by a common carrier against a passenger on account of color. Coger *v.* Northwestern U. Packet Co. (1873). 37 Iowa, 145.)

Constitution, 1857, Article IX. Section 12. The board of education shall provide for the education of all the youths of the state, through a system of common schools.

Constitution, 1857, Article II. Section 1. Voting is limited to white males.

1858

Laws, 1858, Chapter 52. Section 30, Sub-division 4. Colored youths must be in separate schools, except in districts with unanimous consent of persons sending children to school in the district. (Held unconstitutional, 1858, in The District *v.* City of Dubuque, 7 Iowa, 262, which held that the expression "all youths," in Constitution, 1857, Article 9, Section 12, prohibited any distinction being made between white and colored children.)

1864

Laws, 1864, p. 6. Repeal of law of 1851 prohibiting immigration of free negroes.

1868

Laws, 1868, p. 290. The word "white" was stricken from Constitution by legislature. Submitted to popular vote and ratified.

1870

Laws, 1870, p. 21. The right to practice law was extended to women and members of all races.

1884

Laws, 1884, p. 107. (*Civil Rights Law.*) All persons are entitled to the full and equal enjoyment of the accommodations and privileges of inns, public conveyances, barber-shops, theaters and other places of amusement. Violating the provisions of the act, or inciting others to such violation renders the offender guilty of a misdemeanor.

1892

Laws, 1892, p. 68. Civil Rights Law amended, by adding "Inns, restaurants, chop-houses, eating-houses, lunch-counters, and all other places where refreshments are served, and bath-houses."

After such amendment the act read, "Inns, restaurants, chop-houses, eating-houses, lunch-counters, and all other places where refreshments are served, public conveyances, barber-shops, bath-houses, theaters, and all other places of public amusement. Violation is a misdemeanor." (Code, 1897, Section 5008, p. 1956.)

Kansas

1855

Constitution, 1855, Article II. Section 2. Suffrage extended to white persons and to civilized Indians (Negroes not included). Topeka Constitution.

Laws, 1855, Chapter 108, p. 414. First Territorial Legislature. Marriage between white persons and negroes or mulattoes is forbidden and is illegal and void.

1859

Laws, 1859, Chapter 93. Repealed law of 1855, Chapter 108, p. 414, forbidding intermarriage.

1862

Comp. Laws, 1862, Chapter 46, Article IV. Section 18 (*Original*). Cities of not less than 7,000. All taxes for school purposes from black or mulatto persons shall be used for the benefit of the children of such persons, in schools separate and apart from schools authorized for the children of white persons.

1868

General Statutes, 1868, Chapter 18, Article 5. Section 75. Boards of education of cities of the first class (over 150,000) are given "power to organize and maintain separate schools for the education of white and of colored children."

1874

Laws, 1874, p. 82. (*General Statutes, 1909, Section 2916.*) If any trustees, etc., of any state university, college, or other school of public instruction, or those in charge of any inn, hotel or boarding-house, or any place of entertainment or amusement for which a license is required by any of the municipal authorities of this state, or those in charge of any steamboat, railroad, stagecoach, omnibus, street car, or any other means of public carriage for persons or freight shall make any distinction on account of race, color, or previous condition of servitude, it shall be a misdemeanor, punishable by a fine of not less than $10 nor more than $1,000, and the offender shall also be liable in damages to the person injured thereby.

All fines collected by virtue of this act shall be paid over to the public school fund of the county in which the offense is committed.

1876

Laws, 1876, p. 238. Revision of School Law. Omitted the provision of Laws, 1868, Chapter 18, Article 5, Section 75, as to Boards of Education.

Laws, 1876, p. 269. Section 29. Cities of the second class shall have free schools, free to all children.

1879

Laws, 1879, p. 163, Chapter 1. Amendment to School Law. Cities of first class may separate races in schools, except in the high school, where no discrimination shall be made on account of color.

1889

Laws, 1889, p. 329. Public schools in the City of Wichita, a city of the first class. Section 4. No discrimination in the high school shall be made on account of race or color.

1905

Laws, 1905, Chapter 414. Section 1. Schools in Kansas City, Kansas, may organize and maintain separate schools for education of white and colored children, including high schools; but no discrimination on account of color shall be made in high schools, except as provided herein.

Kentucky

1852

Laws, 1852, p. 603. Schools admit "free white children."

1865

Laws, 1865–1866, p. 31. Homestead Act. Homesteads of $1,000 in value shall be exempt from execution or taxation. Section 6 provides that this act shall only apply to white persons.

Laws, 1865–1866, p. 38. A negro can testify only where negroes are parties.

1865–1866

Laws, 1865–1866, p. 37. All colored persons living together as husband and wife, and who continue to do so, are regarded as legally married and their children legitimate. Must appear before clerk of county court, and declare they had been living as husband and wife and wished to continue so.

1866

General Laws, 1866, p. 735. All negroes may sue, acquire property, etc., in the same manner as white persons. Negroes shall be competent witnesses in civil proceedings where negroes are the only parties, and in criminal proceedings where the negro is defendant.

General Laws, 1866, p. 735. It is prohibited for any white person to intermarry with any negro or any descendant of any negro to the third generation inclusive, though one ancestor of each generation was a white person. Such intermarriage shall be a felony, punishable by imprisonment in the state penitentiary not more than five years. (See Revised Statutes, 1852, p. 384.)

General Laws, 1866, p. 736. All persons without distinction of color are declared subject to the same penalties for offenses, except that the laws for the punishment of negroes for rape on white women are continued.

General Laws, 1866, p. 738. The trustees of a school district may cause a separate school to be taught for the education of negro children.

1867

Laws, 1867, p. 94. Negro capitation taxes, and also a special tax of $2 per capita upon negroes, shall be used for the benefit of negro paupers and for the education of negro children.

1869

Laws, 1869, p. 7. A tax on white property for white schools, is provided.

Laws, 1869, p. 127. The school trustees are to encourage indigent white children to attend school.

Laws, 1869, p. 52. Law against rape, applied only to white women. No mention of negro women.

1871–1872

Laws, 1871–1872, p. 7. Section 6 of Act to exempt homesteads from sale for debt (Laws, 1865–1866, p. 31) is amended so as hereafter to extend the provisions of said act to every bona fide house-keeper with a family within this commonwealth, irrespective of race or color.

1873

Laws, 1873–1874, p. 63. A uniform system of common schools for the education of colored children is established. A school fund is created known as the colored school fund, to consist of taxes and fines of negroes, and of donations. No school district shall contain more than one hundred or less than twenty colored children. There shall be three colored school trustees in each district who shall have the management of colored schools. Appeals from them may be taken to the county commissioner. It is unlawful for a colored child to attend a white school, and the reverse. No colored school shall be located within one mile of a white school, except in cities and towns, where it may not be within six hundred feet.

1876

Laws, 1876, p. 112. Separation in lunatic asylums provided for Negro lunatics must not be kept in the same buildings as white lunatics.

1891

Laws, 1891–1892–1893. Common School Act, Article XIV, p. 1,490. Colored school trustees shall be elected in the same manner as white trustees. No tax shall be levied upon property or any services required of any white person for benefit of schools for colored children, and the reverse. It is not lawful for white children to attend colored schools, and the reverse. Colored school officers and teachers are authorized to organize teachers institutes for themselves, like white institutes.

Constitution, 1891, Article VI. Section 187. In distributing school funds no distinction shall be made on account of race or color, and separate schools for white and colored children shall be maintained.

1892

Laws, 1891–1892–1893, p. 63. Any railroad company, steam or otherwise, on any railway line or track within state, shall provide separate coaches for white and colored persons, a good and substantial wooden apartment being deemed a separate coach. They must have signs stating the race for which they are set apart.

There shall be no discrimination in quality of accommodations for white and colored passengers.

Any railway failing to comply with this act shall be fined from $500 to $1,500.

Conductors shall assign passengers to place, if they refuse to go, the conductor may eject them and no damages shall accrue.

Any conductor failing to enforce this law shall be fined from $50 to $100.

This is not to apply to employees of railways, or persons employed as nurses, or officers in charge of prisoners.

1893

Laws, 1893, p. 925. (*Code, 1915, Section 2097*). Marriage is prohibited and declared void between a white person and a negro or mulatto.

Laws, 1893, p. 963. A normal school for colored persons was established, and a department for the education of colored students in agriculture and mechanical arts.

1894

Laws, 1894, March 10. Donations and gifts for education of colored children shall be used for that purpose. A census of colored children between six years and twenty years shall be taken. Repeats provisions of school law of 1891–1892–1893, p. 1,490.

Laws, 1894, p. 157. Separate coach law amended. Adds to exceptions the transportation of passengers in any caboose car attached to a freight train.

1898

Laws, 1898, p. 102. Where, during time of slavery, in Kentucky, colored persons lived together as husband and wife, the children are legitimate. Where a parent subsequently intermarried with another colored person and had children, the slave children shall share in the proportion of their number to the number from the subsequent marriage.

1904

Laws, 1904, p. 129. The property of one race must not be taxed for the support of schools of the other race.

Laws, 1904, p. 181. (*Berea College Act.*) *Section 1.* It shall be unlawful for any person, corporation or association of persons to maintain or operate any college, school or institution where persons of the white and negro races are both received as pupils for instruction; and any person or corporation who shall operate or maintain any such college, school or institution shall be fined $1,000, and any person or corporation who may be convicted of violating the provisions of this act shall be fined $100 for each day they may operate said school, college or institution after such conviction.

Section 2. Any instructor who shall teach in any school, college, or institution where members of said two races are received as pupils for instruction shall be guilty of operating and maintaining same and fined as provided in the first section hereof.

Section 3. It shall be unlawful for any white person to attend any school or institution where negroes are received as pupils or receive instruction, and it shall be unlawful for any negro or colored person to attend any school or institution where white persons are received as pupils or receive instruction. Any person so offending shall be fined $50 for each day he attends such institution or school; provided, that the provisions of this law shall not apply to any penal institution or house of reform.

Section 4. Nothing in this act shall be construed to prevent any private school, college or institution of learning from maintaining a separate and distinct branch thereof, in a different locality, not less than twenty-five miles distant, for the education exclusively of one race or color.

Section 5. This act shall not take effect, or be in operation, before the 15th of July, 1904.

1906

Berea College v. Commonwealth, 123 Kentucky, 209 (1906). So much of statute (*Laws, 1904, p. 181, Berea College act*), as imposes punishment for operating an institution of learning in which white and colored persons may be taught at same time and in same place, is valid; so much as prohibits the operation by any institution of learning of separate branches for white and colored persons less than twenty-five miles distant from each other, is void.

Laws, 1906, p. 315. It is unlawful to present or participate in, or permit any play based upon antagonism alleged formerly to exist between master and slave, or that excites race prejudice. Violating this act is punishable by a fine from $100 to $500, or imprisonment in the country jail one to three months, or both.

1909

Code, 1909. Section 282. An institution for education of colored deaf mutes is established at Donville, under same board as white institution. "But the two races shall be forever kept entirely separate and distinct from each other."

Statutes (*Carroll*), *1909, p. 1,240. Section 5112.* Colored blind children are cared for in the Kentucky Institution for the Education of the Blind.

1910

Acts, 1910, p. 207. All negroes and mulattoes living together as husband and wife prior to February 14, 1866, and continuing since till the death of either or both, or still continuing if living, are legally married and their issue legitimate. The customary marriages and issue of same of negroes and mulattoes prior to February 14, 1866, are legitimate. (Broader than 1898 Laws, p. 102.)

Acts, 1910, p. 277. "Whereas some difficulty has arisen in construing various acts appropriating funds for the benefit of schools for the white and colored deaf," a school for white deaf and a school for colored deaf is established to be maintained and operated as separate and distinct institutions but under the same superintendent and the same Board of Commissioners.

1915

Statutes (*Carroll*), *1915. Section 4487.* The provisions of the common school law shall apply to such graded common school districts as may be applied for and organized by the colored people of this Commonwealth. The word colored is to be substituted for the word white. No white person shall vote at any election held by colored people under provisions of this law, nor shall property of any white person be taxed to maintain any graded common school for colored children and vice versa, nor shall any white child attend any graded common school for colored children and vice versa.

Louisiana

1868

Acts, 1868, p. 278; Revised Statutes, 1870, p. 436. Section 2212. Legalized all marriages, provided that parties within two years make a declaration of their marriage before a notary or other proper officer, giving the date of marriage and the number and age of children.

Constitution, 1868, Title VII, Article 135. There shall be no separate schools or institutions of learning established exclusively for any race. (For a previous provision to the contrary see Constitution, 1845, Title VII, and Constitution, 1852, Title VIII.)

Constitution, 1868, Title 6, Article 98. Removed limitation of suffrage to white persons.

1869

Acts, 1869, p. 37, Code of 1870, Section 456. (See 1914.) Against discrimination. Common carriers shall have the right to refuse to admit any person to their railroad cars, street cars, steamboats or other water craft, coaches, omnibusses, or other vehicles, or to expel any person therefrom for refusal to pay fare, or a person of infamous character, or one guilty of disorderly conduct, or any one who shall commit any act tending to injure the business of the carrier, prescribed for the management of his business after such rules and regulations shall have been made known. Provided, that said rules and regulations make no discrimination on account of race or color.

Except in the cases enumerated in this act no person shall be refused admission to or entertainment at any public inn, hotel, or place of public resort.

All licenses hereafter granted to persons engaged in business or keeping places of public resort, shall contain the express condition that places of business or public resort shall be open to the accommodation and patronage of all persons with no discrimination on account of race or color. The penalty for violation shall be the forfeiture of the license and closing of the place of business or of public resort; and moreover, the offender shall be liable at the suit of the person aggrieved to such damages as he shall sustain thereby. In case of violation of the provisions of this act, the injured party shall have the right to recover damages, exemplary as well as actual.

1870

Revised Code, 1870. Section 2215. The right of making private or religious marriages legal, valid, and binding shall apply to all persons of whatever race or color as well as to marriages formerly prohibited by any law of the state.

Section 2216. Any parties who at any time previous to the passage of this act lived together as man and wife, and who desire to contract a legal marriage, shall be entitled to the benefit of the provisions of this law.

Revised Code, 1870. Nothing found against intermarriage or miscegenation, under those headings, or any other headings.

1871

Laws, 1871, p. 57. The mode of trying cases arising under the Civil Rights Act of 1869, p. 37, is provided for.

Laws, 1871, p. 208. Provision for the instruction of the blind, and for an industrial home for the blind at Baton Rouge. Provides that "no part of this act shall be construed so as to deprive any person on account of race or color of the privilege of admittance to the institution."

1873

Laws, 1873, p. 156. Every citizen of Louisiana and of the United States residing in Louisiana, shall enjoy equal and impartial accommodations, advantages, facilities, and privileges from all common carriers on land and water, from inn-keepers and from all public places of resort licensed by the state or by any municipal corporation.

If any inn-keeper or manager of public resort refuse equal and impartial accommodations to any citizen, he shall forfeit his license and thereafter shall not pursue that calling and shall be liable to the injured party for damages. Common carriers are liable on an action for damages in favor of the injured party, and each carrier shall forfeit license.

The Attorney-General on complaint shall take proceedings in the name of the state and preference shall be given to his proceeding.

If any agent of a railroad or steamboat company shall thus discriminate, such employee shall be arrested and fined or imprisoned, and shall be liable for damages in favor of the person so injured. (See 1902 for repeal.)

1875

Hall v. DeCuir, 97 United States 485. Held Act of 1869 against discrimination by railroads, etc., unconstitutional, because it constituted interference with interstate commerce.

Laws, 1875, p. 50. Establishment of an agricultural and mechanical college. It is provided there shall be no discrimination of race or color in the admission, management, or discipline of the institution.

1879

Constitution. No reference is made either way as to separation in schools. The provision of the 1868 Constitution is omitted.

1880

Laws, 1880, p. 52. There shall be no distinction made on account of race, color, or previous condition of servitude, in selecting jurors.

Laws, 1880, p. 110. Provides for the establishment of Southern University, for the education of negroes.

1890

Laws, 1890, p. 152. (*Code, 1904, p. 1498.*) Railway companies shall provide equal but separate accommodations for white and colored races by providing two or more coaches, or by partition in coach. This Act shall not apply to street railroads. No person shall occupy any seat other than the one assigned.

Section 2. Officers shall assign passengers to proper seats. Persons insisting on entering wrong place may be fined $25, or imprisoned for not more than twenty days. A railroad officer assigning any one to improper place may be punished by fine of $25 or imprisonment not exceeding twenty days. A passenger refusing to occupy the proper place may be ejected. No liability for damages by railway company for so doing shall be incurred.

Section 3. All officers and directors of railway companies that shall refuse or neglect to comply with the provisions and requirements of this Act shall be deemed guilty of a misdemeanor and shall upon conviction before any court of competent jurisdiction be fined not less than $100 nor more than $500, and any conductor or other employee of such passenger train who shall refuse or neglect to carry out the provisions of this Act shall on conviction be fined not less than $25 nor more than $50 for each offense. All railroad companies other than street railroad companies shall keep this law posted in a conspicuous place in each passenger coach and ticket office. Nothing herein shall be construed as applying to nurses travelling with children of other race, or officers in charge of prisoners.

1894

Laws, 1894, p. 63. Marriage between white persons and persons of color is prohibited, and its celebration is forbidden, and it is null and void. (No special penalty attached. Only penalty that for any marriage within forbidden degrees).

Laws, 1894, p. 200. Amends separate coach law of 1890, p. 152, by adding to Section 3 the words, "or prisoners in charge of sheriffs or their deputies or other officers."

Laws, 1894, p. 133. (*Revised Statutes, 1904, p. 1500.*) Upon the construction or renewal of depots, they must have equal but separate waiting rooms for the white and colored races. No person shall occupy the wrong room.

Section 2. The power to assign any one to the proper place is given to railroad employees. Any person insisting on entering the improper place may be fined $25 or imprisoned not more than 30 days. An agent assigning any one to improper place may be fined $25 or imprisoned not more than 30 days. Upon refusal of any person to occupy an assigned place, he may be ejected, with no liability for damages.

Section 3. An agent failing to enforce this Act is guilty of a misdemeanor, punishable by $25 to $50 fine. This law must be posted in a conspicuous place. Nurses attending children of other race and sheriffs having persons in charge are made exceptions.

1898

Constitution, 1898, Article 248. The General Assembly shall establish free public schools for the white and the colored races.

1902

Laws, 1902, p. 89. All street railways must provide separate but equal accommodations, consisting of two cars, or else of wooden or wire screen partitions.

Section 2. Railway officers must assign passengers to the proper seat. A passenger insisting on going to a wrong seat is liable to a fine of $25 or imprisonment of not more than thirty days. A railway officer making an improper assignment is liable to a fine of $25 or imprisonment for not more than thirty days. A passenger refusing to occupy the proper place may be ejected, with no damages from the railway company.

Section 3. For a railway company refusing to comply with these provisions, a penalty is provided of a fine of $100, or imprisonment for not less than sixty days and not more than six months. A conductor not enforcing the Act is fined not less than $25 or imprisoned not less than ten days and not more than thirty days. The law shall be posted in a conspicuous place in cars and stations. Exception to the law is made of nurses attending children of the other race.

Laws, 1902, p. 27. Repeal of Civil Rights Act of 1873, p. 156.

Laws, 1902, p. 144, Act to establish the "Insane Asylum for Colored People of the State of Louisiana."

1904

Laws, 1904, p. 353. A requirement to keep separate as far as practicable males under eighteen years of the white and colored races, in the Reform School (Louisiana Training Institute).

1908

Act 87, p. 105. Concubinage between the Caucasian or white race and any person of the negro or black race is a felony. The punishment is imprisonment from one month to one year, with or without hard labor.

Section 2. Living together is proof of violation of this act.

Laws, 1908, p. 239. It is unlawful for any person conducting a barroom, cabaret, coffee-house, cafe, beer-saloon, liquor exchange, drinking grog-shop, beer-house, beer-garden, or other place where spirituous, vinous or malt liquors or intoxicating beverages are sold, to permit in same building the sale for consumption on the premises of intoxicating liquors to whites and negroes. Violation is a misdemeanor, punishable by $50 to $500 fine, or imprisonment in the parish jail or the parish prison not more than two years, or both.

1910

Laws, 1910, p. 32. Same as 1908, p. 239, except that the words are used "Persons of the Caucasian and colored races."

Laws, 1910, p. 344. Law of 1908, p. 105, as to concubinage repeated, changing the word "negro" to the word "color" or "colored."

1912

Laws, 1912, p. 139. Municipal corporations are authorized to withhold building permits for building negro houses in white communities, or any portion of a community inhabited principally by white people, and vice versa, except on the written consent of a majority of those of the opposite race in the portion to be effected.

Section 2. The words "white community" and "negro community" mean any subdivision or portion thereof, or any street, inhabited principally by white people, or vice versa, as case may be.

Section 3. A firm or person violating these provisions, by building such a house without a permit is liable to a fine of from $50 to $2,000, and the municipality shall have the right to cause said building to be removed and destroyed.

1914

Annotated Revised Statutes, 1914. Civil Rights Law of 1869, as Sections 922–925.

Maine

1819

Constitution, 1819, II. Every male citizen had the right to vote.

1821

Laws, 1821, Vol. I, p. 341. All marriages between white persons and negroes, mulattoes, or Indians are prohibited. Any such marriage shall be absolutely void.

1847

Revised Statutes, 1847, Chapter 59. Section 3. The same provision appears, as to intermarriage. (This is the last Revised Statutes in which this provision appears. It is not contained in the next edition of the Revised Statutes in 1857. It was not repealed till as appears below).

1883

Laws, 1883, p. 167. The law as to marriage is amended by striking out the provision as to marriages of whites with negroes, etc. Repeals law of 1821.

Maryland

1867

Constitution, 1867, Article III. Section 1. (Constitution not changed since.) "White male citizens" have the right to vote.

Constitution, 1867, Article III. Section 53. No person shall be incompetent as a witness unless thereafter so declared by general assembly.

Chapter 423, p. 858. Marriages made in the state prior to March 22, 1867, between colored people, are confirmed and made valid from time of celebration, and are good and sufficient in law. The parties claiming to have been married shall establish the fact before some Justice of Peace, a certificate of which shall be filed with the clerk of the circuit court for the county or the Court of Common Pleas of Baltimore City.

Thereafter, colored persons are to be married in the same manner and under same regulations as white persons.

1870

Laws, 1870, Chapter 392. Section 1. The House of Reformation for colored minors is provided for (like the House of Refuge for white minors, with the same provisions as in chapter as to latter).

Laws, 1870, p. 555–556. All taxes paid for school purposes by colored people in any county or in the city of Baltimore, and donations for that purpose, shall be set aside for maintaining schools for colored children. Further appropriations can be made by school commissioners.

1872

Laws, 1872, p. 650. The Board of County School Commissioners shall establish schools for colored children in each election district, subject to same laws and regulations as schools for white children. The taxes of colored persons shall be devoted to them except that no colored school shall be established in a district unless the colored population warrants.

Laws, 1872, Chapter 377, p. 650. The Board of County School Commissioners shall establish one or more public schools in each election district for all colored youth between six and twenty years of age, admission to be free provided the colored population of such district shall warrant in establishing said schools.

Laws, 1872, Chapter 377. Colored schools are provided with support from the general school fund.

Laws, 1872, p. 134. Admission to the bar is limited to white male citizens.

Laws, 1872, Chapter 377. The taxes paid for school purposes by the colored people of any county shall be used for schools for colored children.

1874

Laws, 1874, Chapter 463, p. 690. Colored schools shall be under the direction of a special Board of School Trustees, subject to the same laws for their government, and furnished with instruction in the same branches, as schools for white children.

1876

Laws, 1876, p. 469. Admission to the bar is limited to white male citizens.

1882

Laws, 1882, Chapter 291. Section 1. An industrial home for colored girls is authorized.

1884

Laws, 1884, Chapter 264. All marriages between white persons and negroes or white persons and persons of negro descent to third generation inclusive, are forever prohibited, and void. Such person is guilty of infamous crime and subject to a penalty of imprisonment in the penitentiary for not less than eighteen months nor more than ten years.

Any minister or other person joining in marriage any negro with any white person shall be fined $100. (See Code, 1860, p. 236 and p. 241, and Laws, 1715, Chapter 44, Section 25.)

1894

Laws, 1894, p. 939, Chapter 187. Section 329A. The House of the Good Shepherd for colored girls of the city of Baltimore is provided for. A refuge for colored females wishing to abandon vicious courses and reform. It is vested with same powers and duties as by law for white females and the House of the Good Shepherd of the city of Baltimore.

All courts and Justices of Peace can commit colored females in the same way as white females to the latter institution.

1898

Laws, 1898, p. 815. The Board of County School Commissioners, wherever suitable accommodations are provided by the County, shall provide for the maintenance of separate colored industrial schools if in their judgment needed, the salaries to be paid out of the general fund.

1904

Laws, 1904, p. 240. In 1904 Maryland laws, race qualifications are omitted for admission to the bar. (See 1914.)

Laws, 1904, p. 186, Chapter 109. Section 1. All railroad companies are required to provide separate cars or coaches for white and colored passengers; a compartment with a "good and substantial partition with a door or place of exit from each division" is compliance. They must have words in plain letters in a conspicuous place indicating whether for white or colored passengers.

Section 2. There must be no difference or discrimination in quality of convenience or accommodation.

Section 3. Any railroad company or person failing to comply with this act may be fined not less than $300 nor more than $1,000 for each offense.

Section 4. Conductors shall assign to each white or colored passenger his place and may eject a passenger refusing to occupy the place assigned, neither railroad company or conductor being liable in damages. The passenger refusing to occupy the assigned place is guilty of a misdemeanor and fined not less than $5 nor more than $50, or imprisoned in the jail not less than thirty days, or both.

Section 5. Any conductor who shall fail to perform the duties in Section 4 is guilty of a misdemeanor and fined not less than $25 nor more than $50.

Section 6. When either section is completely filled, and this could not be foreseen, and no extra cars can be obtained, the conductor may assign passengers of one color to the place for the other.

Section 7. These provisions shall not apply to employees of railroads or persons employed as nurses or officers in charge of prisoners, whether white or colored or both, or to prisoners in their custody, nor to transportation of passengers in a caboose car attached to a freight train, nor to parlor nor sleeping cars, nor through express trains that do no local business.

Laws, 1904, Chapter 110. Section 1. Officers of steamboats shall assign white and colored passengers to the respective locations they are to occupy. They must separate as far as the construction of boat and due consideration for comfort of passengers will permit, white and colored passengers in sitting, sleeping, and eating apartments. No discrimination shall be made in quality and convenience of accommodations in the respective locations. Exceptions to the Act are made of nurses or attendants traveling with employers, officers in charge of prisoners, white or colored, or both, and to prisoners in their custody.

Section 2. An officer in command of any boat refusing to enforce this Act, is guilty of a misdemeanor, and fined not less than $25 nor more than $50.

Section 3. A passenger refusing to occupy the location assigned, whether of sitting, sleeping, or eating, is guilty of misdemeanor, and may be fined not less than $5 nor more than $50, or imprisoned in jail not less than thirty days. He may be ejected from the boat. Necessary assistance to do this may be secured. No liability for damages by the steamboat company or officers shall be incurred.

1908

Laws, 1908, Chapter 248. Conductors or managers of railway companies operating cars by electricity, running twenty miles beyond the limits of any incorporated city or town of the state for transportation of passengers, are required to designate separate seats for white and colored passengers. They shall make no discrimination in quality of or convenience in seats. No white person shall force himself into a seat designated for a colored person (and vice versa). If a passenger refuses to occupy an assigned seat, the conductor may refuse to carry, and may put off, such passengers. He shall not be liable therefor in damages. Such passenger is guilty of a misdemeanor, and may be fined not more than $50, or imprisoned in jail thirty days, or both. A conductor refusing to enforce the act is guilty of a misdemeanor, and may be fined not more than $20. When the seats are all occupied but are not all filled, and an increased number of passengers cannot be accommodated with separate seats, the conductor is authorized to assign passengers of the same color to vacant seats, and with permission of the occupant can assign a passenger of another color to the unoccupied seats, but not otherwise. The act shall not apply to nurses or valets accompanying those needing their attention.

Laws, 1908, Chapter 292. The provision that "Each compartment of a car divided by a good substantial partition, with a door or place of exit from each division, shall be deemed a separate car," shall not be applied to counties of Prince George's, Charles, St. Mary's, Calvert, and Anne Arundel, so that in said counties there shall be separate cars or coaches. But a combination car, not over one-third of which is used for baggage or mail, for the purposes of this section shall be deemed a separate car. Each separate car shall have in a conspicuous place, both inside and outside, words and letters indicating whether set apart for white or colored passengers. This section shall not apply to trains making no scheduled intermediate service stops between their termini.

Laws, 1908, Chapter 617. Steamboats on Chesapeake Bay, between the City of Baltimore and points on the Bay and its tributaries, shall provide separate toilet or retiring rooms, and separate sleeping cabins, on or before July 1, 1908, for white and colored passengers, under penalty of $50 for each day's violation.

Laws 1908, Chapter 599. A State Normal School for instruction and practice of colored teachers is authorized, under the control of the State Board of Education. It shall include courses for preparation for teaching elements of agricultural and mechanical arts, etc.

1910

Laws, 1910, p. 232. The Colored Industrial School law of 1848 is amplified and made more specific.

Laws, 1910, p. 238. Establishes a "hospital for the negro insane of Maryland," for the detention and care of the negro insane of the state.

1914

Chapter 655, p. 1108. All persons possessing the necessary qualifications shall be eligible to take examinations for admission to the bar.

Massachusetts

1705

Laws, 1705, Chapter 6. An Act for the better preventing of spurious and mixed issue. A negro or "molatto" man committing fornication with "an English woman or a woman of any other Christian nation," shall be sold out of the province. An "English man, or man of any other Christian nation," committing fornication with a negro or molatto woman, shall be whipped, and the woman sold out of the province.

None of Her Majesty's English or Scottish subjects nor of any other Christian nation within this province "shall contract matrimony with any negro or molatto" under a penalty imposed on the person joining them in marriage.

1784

Laws, 1784, p. 72. Section 10. Whoever confines or imprisons without lawful authority another person against his will, or kidnaps another person, and whoever sells or in any manner transfers for any term the service or labor of a negro, mulatto, or other person of color, who has been unlawfully seized or kidnapped from here to any other state or place, shall be punished by imprisonment of not more than ten years, or a fine of not more than $1,000 and imprisonment in jail of not more than two years. Whoever commits any offense described in this section to extort money or other valuable thing, shall be punished by an imprisonment in the State Prison not more than twenty-five years. (1902 Revised Laws, Chapter 207, Section 26.)

1786

Laws, 1786, Chapter 3. Section 7. No person authorized to marry shall join in marriage any white person with any negro, Indian, or mulatto, under the penalty of £50; and all such marriages shall be absolutely null and void.

1788

Laws, 1788, Chapter 2, March 26. No African or negro other than a citizen of one of the States shall tarry in the Commonwealth more than two months, or he may be ordered to depart, and if he does not depart he may be subject to penalty.

1834

Laws, 1834, Chapter 177. An act for the orderly solemnization of marriage, repealing former acts, but excepting Section 7 of Act of 1786.

1843

Laws, 1843, Chapter 5. An act relating to marriages between individuals of certain races. This act repeals the provisions against the intermarriage of whites, negroes, etc.

1855

Acts, 1855, p. 674, Chapter 256. (*School Act.*) No distinction shall be made on account of race, color, or religious opinions of the applicant or scholar.

Section 2. Any child who on account of his race, color, or religious opinions is excluded from any public or district school may recover damages in an action of tort.

Section 4. Every person belonging to a school committee under whose rules any child shall be excluded, and the teacher of any such school, shall, on application by the parent or guardian, state in writing the grounds and reasons of such exclusion.

1865

Acts, 1865, p. 650. No distinction, discrimination, or restriction on account of color or race shall be lawful in any licensed inn, in any public place of amusement, public conveyance, or public meeting. Penalty, a fine not exceeding $50.

1866

Acts, 1866, p. 242. It is not lawful to exclude persons from or restrict them in any theater or public place of amusement, licensed under the laws of the Commonwealth, or in any public conveyance or public meeting, or licensed inn, except for good cause. Penalty, a fine not exceeding $50.

1884

Laws, 1884, p. 194. No life insurance company shall make any distinction between white and colored persons wholly or partially of African descent, as to premiums or rates, or as to amount to be paid in case of death, nor insert in the policy any condition as to accepting less than full value of the policy, other than such as are imposed upon white persons in similar cases.

Any such company which shall refuse an application of a colored person for insurance upon his life, shall furnish, on request, the certificate of the doctor of the company stating that the refusal is not on account of color but solely upon such grounds of general health and prospect of longevity as would be applicable to white persons of the same age and sex.

Any corporation or officer or agent violating the provisions of this Act, shall forfeit not to exceed $100.

1885

Acts, 1885, p. 774. There shall be no distinction or discrimination on account of color or race, or except for good cause, in admission to or treatment in any theater, skating-rink, or other public place of amusement, whether licensed or not, or public conveyance, public meeting or inn, whether licensed or not. Penalty, a fine not exceeding $100.

1887

Acts, 1887, p. 815. Section 69. Same as insurance act of 1884, p. 194, but Section 3 (penalty) omitted.

1893

Acts; 1893, p. 1320. Added after inn in 1885 Acts, p. 774, "barber's shop or other public place kept for hire, gain, or reward."

1894

Acts, 1894, p. 825. A resolution deprecating the action of the National League of American Wheelmen in voting to exclude colored persons from membership.

Acts, 1894, p. 609. Section 11. No person shall be excluded from a public school on account of race, color, or the religious opinions of the applicant or scholar.

1895

Acts, 1895, p. 519. Whoever makes any distinction, discrimination, or restriction on account of color or race, or except for good cause, applicable alike to all persons of every color and race, relative to the admission of any person to or his treatment in, a theater, skating-rink, or other place of amusement, licensed or unlicensed, or in a public conveyance or public meeting, or in an inn, barber shop, or other public place kept for hire, gain, or reward, licensed or unlicensed, or whoever aids or incites such a distinction, shall for each offense be punished by a fine of not more than $300 or imprisonment for not more than one year, or both, and shall forfeit to any person aggrieved thereby not less than $25 nor more than $300, but such person so aggrieved shall not recover against more than one person by reason of one act.

1896

Acts, 1896, p. 659. A resolution expressing reprobation of hotels in Boston for excluding a colored bishop, the senior bishop of the American Methodist Episcopal Church.

Michigan

1838

Revised Statutes, 1838, p. 334. No white person shall intermarry with a negro or mulatto.

1850

Constitution, 1850, Article VII. Section 1. White males only have the franchise.

1871

Laws, 1871, p. 274. No separate school or department shall be kept for any persons on account of race or color. Provided, That this shall not be construed to prevent the grading of schools according to the intellectual progress of the pupil. (Howell's Statutes, 1913, Section 9904.)

1883

Laws, 1883, p. 16. All marriages heretofore contracted between white persons and those wholly or partly African of descent, are hereby declared valid and effectual in law for all purposes, and the issue of such marriages shall be deemed and taken as legitimate as to such issue and as to both of the parents.

1885

Laws, 1885, p. 131. All persons are entitled to the full and equal accommodations of inns, restaurants, eating-houses, barber shops, public conveyances on land and water, theaters, and all other places of public accommodation and amusement, subject only to the conditions and limitation established by law and applicable alike to all citizens.

Denying the full accommodation or aiding or inciting such denial is a misdemeanor punished by a fine not to exceed $100, or imprisonment for not more than thirty days, or both.

No citizen possessing all other qualifications shall be disqualified to serve as grand or petit juror in any court of the State on account of race or color. Any officer excluding or failing to summon any citizen for such cause, is guilty of misdemeanor and shall be fined not more than $100 or imprisoned not more than thirty days, or both.

1893

Laws, 1893, p. 60. No life insurance company shall make discrimination between white and colored persons, wholly or partially of African descent, as to premiums charged, nor make any rebate or diminution upon the amount paid in case of death, nor insert any condition in a policy for any less sum than full value. There shall be a forfeit to the State of $500 for each violation, to be covered by the attorney-general. Any officer or agent violating the law is guilty of a misdemeanor, and shall be punished by confinement in the county jail not exceeding one year, or by fine not less than $50 and not exceeding $500, or both.

1899

Laws, 1899, p. 387. Marriage law of 1883, p. 16, repeated.

1901

Laws, 1901, p. 293. The Michigan National Guard shall be composed of not less than forty companies of infantry. Provided, That if more than forty companies are organized, at least one shall be composed of colored men.

1905

Laws, 1905, p. 158. The Michigan National Guard shall be composed or not less than thirty-six companies of infantry, and not more than thirty-six companies shall be organized and maintained as part of the Michigan National Guard until after there be organized one troop of cavalry, one battery of light artillery, one signal corps, and one company of engineers. (No mention of colored regiment.)

Minnesota

1857

Constitution, 1857, Article VII. Section 1. White males only given franchise.

1865

Laws, 1865, p. 118. A Constitutional amendment submitted giving negroes the suffrage. Defeated by a vote of the State.

1877

General Laws, 1877, p. 141. (Chapter 74, Chapter 6, Section 1). If children are denied admission to public schools, or suspended or expelled on account of color, social position, or nationality, the board shall forfeit $50 for each offense; and nothing in this act or any amendment to it shall be so construed as to authorize classifying scholars with reference to color, or to set them apart into separate schools without their consent and the consent of the parents or guardians of such children. Any district offending shall lose the benefit of the public school funds.

1885

Laws, 1885, p. 296. All persons shall be entitled to the full and equal enjoyment of the accommodations, advantages, facilities, and privileges of inns, public conveyances on land and water, theaters, and places of public amusement, restaurants, and barber shops, subject only to the conditions and limitations applicable alike to all citizens of every race and color regardless of any previous condition of servitude. Penalty for violation, a fine from $100 to $500, or imprisonment from thirty days to one year.

1897

Laws, 1897, p. 616. (*Civil Rights Law.*) Prohibits excluding from "accommodations furnished by innkeepers, hotel keepers, managers or lessees, common carriers, or by owners, managers or lessees of theaters or other places of amusement, or public conveyances on land or water, restaurants, barber shops, eating houses, or other places of public resort, refreshment, accommodation, or entertainment."

Denying the enjoyment unlawfully of any hotel, inn, tavern, restaurant, eating house, soda-water fountain, ice-cream parlor, public conveyance on land or water, theater, barber shop, or other place of public refreshment, amusement, instruction, accommodation, or entertainment is a misdemeanor with penalty of a fine from $25 to $100, or confinement in a county jail from thirty to ninety days. Damages of from $25 to $500 are provided for the injured party.

1899

Laws, 1899, p. 38. No person shall be excluded on account of race or color from full enjoyment of any accommodation furnished by public conveyances, theaters, or other public places of amusement, or by hotels, barber shops, saloons, restaurants, or other places of refreshment, entertainment, or accommodation. Violation of this act or inciting thereto is a gross misdemeanor, and in addition to the penalty therefor, the offender is made liable to the person aggrieved for damages not exceeding $500.

1905

Revised Laws, 1905, Section 1402. Separate school provision of 1877, General Laws, p. 141, repeated, in substance, with provision as to consent omitted.

Revised Laws, 1905. Section 1403. A school district shall not classify its pupils with reference to race or color, nor separate them into different schools or departments for these reasons. Punishment is forfeiture by a district of its share of the public school fund so long as such classification or separation continues. (General Statutes, 1913, Section 2901.)

Mississippi

1865

Laws, 1865, p. 82. Negroes may intermarry with each other under the same regulations as for white persons. All who have been and are cohabiting are held in law as married and the children as legitimate.

Laws, 1865, p. 82. Section 3. It is not lawful for any freedman, free negro, or mulatto to intermarry with any white person (or vice versa). It is a felony. The penalty is imprisonment in the state penitentiary for life. Those shall be deemed freedmen, free negroes, or mulattoes who are of pure negro blood, and those descended from a negro to the third generation, though one ancestor of each generation may have been a white person. (See Revised Code, 1857, p. 311. Digest Laws, 1839, p. 560.)

Laws, 1865, p. 92. There is the same liability for negroes to support their indigents as for white persons theirs. A tax of $1 is placed upon every freedman, free negro, or mulatto between eighteen and sixty years of age, for the Freedman's Pauper Fund. If they refuse to pay tax, they may be arrested and hired out till the amount is worked out.

Laws, 1865, p. 231. (General Act in Relation to Railroads.) Section 6. It is unlawful for any officer or employee on any railroad to allow any freedman, negro, or mulatto to ride in any first-class passenger cars, set apart, or used by and for white persons. Offending is a misdemeanor punished by a fine from $50 to $500; and imprisonment in county jail until fine and costs of prosecution are paid. Provided this section is not to apply in case of negroes or mulattoes travelling with their mistresses in the capacity of nurses.

Section 8. Half of the fines collected under the Act shall be paid to the informer, the other half into the treasury of the county where the offense was committed.

1867

Laws, 1866–1867, p. 232. Negroes are given the right to testify on the same terms as white persons.

Laws, 1866–1867, p. 233. Negroes are not competent to serve as petit or grand jurors.

1868

Constitution, 1868, Article VII, Section 2. Removed the limitation of suffrage to white persons only.

Constitution, 1868, Article 1. Section 24. The rights of all citizens to travel upon all public conveyances shall not be infringed upon nor in any manner abridged in this State.

1871

Revised Code, Mississippi. No miscegenation or intermarriage statute. Omitted.

Revised Code, 1871. Section 1993. All children from five to twenty-one years of age shall have in all respects equal advantages in public schools. (Only provision in the law.)

1872

66 Tennessee, 9. State v. J. P. Bell. Case of a white man married to a woman of color in the state of Mississippi ("where such marriages are not forbidden by law") who removed to Tennessee with his wife. Held an indictable offense in Tennessee for a white man and colored woman to live together as man and wife, although married according to the forms of law in Mississippi.

Laws, 1872, p. 85. There shall be no distinction on account of race or color or previous condition in working convicts.

1873

Laws, 1873, p. 66. All citizens of the State without distinction of race, color, or previous condition of servitude, are entitled to equal and impartial enjoyment of any accommodation, advantage, or privilege furnished by common carriers, whether upon land or upon water, by any keeper or lessee of any hotel, inn, or restaurant, by any owner or manager of any theater or other place of public amusement or of public entertainment or accommodation, and the equal and impartial enjoyment of such accommodation shall forever remain a right inherent in every person, which right shall not be abridged or denied on account of any distinction of race, color, or previous condition of servitude.

Any person violating or abridging these rights is guilty of a misdemeanor, and shall pay to the person aggrieved not less than $300, with full costs and allowance for counsel's fees, and shall be fined not less than $100, or imprisoned not less than thirty days or more than one year, or both. Any corporation, association, or individual violating the same shall forfeit charter or license. Continuing to operate without a charter or license is a misdemeanor, punishable by a fine of not less than $1,000 and not more than $5,000, and imprisonment of not less than three nor more than seven years for each offense. The corporate and joint property of such corporation, association, or individual shall be liable for the forfeitures, fines, and penalties incurred.

The burden of proof is upon the defendant to show the refusal was not on account of race, color, or previous condition of servitude. Judges of circuit courts shall give this Act specially in charge to the grand jury. District attorneys shall prosecute such cases. Any district attorney refusing is guilty of a misdemeanor in office, punishable by $500 to $1,000 fine and may also be dismissed from office.

1878

Laws, 1878, p. 103. It is prohibited to teach white and colored children in the same schoolhouse.

Laws, 1878, p. 119. Section 1. The Alcorn Agricultural and Mechanical College of Mississippi is authorized, for education of colored youth of the State. Provisions same in substance as those for

Mississippi Agricultural and Mechanical College (white), one-half of interest on State fund going to each institution.

1880

Revised Code, 1880. Section 1147. Marriage is unlawful between white persons and negroes or mulattoes or persons of one-quarter or more negro blood, and is incestuous and void.

The punishment is the same as for marriage within prohibited degrees, namely, a fine up to $500, or imprisonment in the penitentiary up to ten years, or both. (Reinsertion of law omitted in 1871. Not found in Session Laws, 1873–1890.)

1888

Laws, 1888, p. 45. Section 2. (General Act as to Railroad Commission, etc.) The Board is authorized to designate and provide, "if deemed proper, separate rooms for the sexes and the races," in any new depot building.

Section 3. Every conductor of trains carrying passengers is authorized to assign passengers to any car, or to seats in a particular part of any car on his train, provided that equal accommodations are given to passengers holding tickets of same class, and any forcible resistance to such assignment is deemed a breach of the peace.

Laws, 1888, p. 48. All railroads carrying passengers (other than street railways) shall provide equal but separate accommodation for the white and colored races, by providing two or more passenger cars for each passenger train, or by dividing the passenger cars by a partition so as to secure separate accommodations.

Section 2. Conductors of passenger trains are required to assign each passenger to the car or compartment of car (when divided by a partition) used for the race to which the passenger belongs. A passenger refusing to occupy car assigned may be refused transportation, and the company shall not be liable for damages.

Section 3. Railroad companies neglecting within sixty days after approval of act to comply with this law are guilty of a misdemeanor, and may be fined not more than $500. A conductor failing to enforce the law may be fined from $25 to $50 for each offense.

1890

Constitution, 1890, Article VIII. Section 207. Separate schools shall be maintained for children of the white and colored races.

Constitution, 1890, Article XIV. Section 263. The marriage of a white person with a negro or mulatto or person who shall have one-eighth or more of negro blood shall be null and void.

Laws, 1890, p. 58. A lunatic asylum is established, with an annex for colored patients. The white and colored races shall be kept separate.

1896

Laws, 1896, p. 115. Separate districts shall be made for the schools of the white and colored races, and the districts for each race shall embrace the whole territory of the county outside the separate school districts.

1904

Laws, 1904, p. 140. All street railways carrying passengers shall provide equal but separate accommodations for the white and colored races by providing two or more cars or by dividing their cars by a partition or by adjustable screens which may be made movable so as to allow adjustment of space in the car suited to the requirements of traffic, so as to secure separate accommodations for white and colored races. No persons are permitted to occupy seats in a car or compartment other than those assigned to them on account of the race to which they belong.

Section 2. Employees on street cars are required to assign passengers to their places. A passenger insisting on occupying a wrong place is liable to a fine of $25 or confinement not more than thirty days in county jail. An employee insisting on assigning passenger to compartment other than proper one, is liable to a fine of $25 or confinement not more than thirty days in the county jail. If a passenger refuse to occupy proper place, the company may refuse to carry him, and no damages against either employee or railway company may be collected.

Section 3. A street railway not complying with these provisions is guilty of a misdemeanor, the penalty being a fine of not less than $100, or imprisonment not less than sixty days and not more than six months. Employees not carrying out the provisions of this act may be fined not less than $25, or imprisoned not more than thirty days. Street railways shall keep the law posted in a conspicuous place in each car and at transfer stations.

An exception is made of nurses attending children of the other race.

1906

Code, 1906. Section 1351. A railroad failing to provide two passenger cars, or a partition, for separate accommodation for the white and colored races; or a conductor failing to assign a passenger to his proper place, is guilty of a misdemeanor. Fine $20 to $500.

Code, 1906. Section 4866. It is the duty of the railroad commission to require comfortable and suitable waiting-rooms for passengers, separate for the races.

Code, 1906. Section 4855. In cities of 3,000 or more inhabitants, the commission shall cause to be maintained in connection with the reception-room for whites, two closets or retiring-rooms with notice painted on doors, "Closet, white, females only," "Closet, white, males only." Likewise closets shall be provided for negroes with like signs painted on the doors, substituting "colored" for "white."

Code, 1906. Section 3244. The marriage of a white person with a negro or mulatto or a person with one-eighth or more of negro blood, or with a Mongolian or person with one-eighth or more of Mongolian blood, is unlawful and void.

Code, 1906. Section 1031. Persons being within the degrees within which marriages are declared by law to be incestuous and void, cohabiting, or committing adultery, etc., are liable to a penalty of imprisonment not exceeding ten years.

Code, 1906. Section 3625. In the penitentiary, white convicts shall have separate apartments from the negro convicts, for both eating and sleeping.

1908

Laws, 1908, p. 186. In no case shall male and female nor white and colored convicts be allowed to sleep in the same apartment, or where they can have access to each other, and as far as practicable they must be worked separately.

Missouri

1865

Laws, 1864, p. 68. All persons of color claiming to be married and wishing to continue so, must be remarried. A list of the children shall be recorded by the reputed father and mother of children.

Laws, 1864, p. 126. Strikes out word "white" from school laws and makes provision for the instruction of all children, provided they are sent to separate schools. (Law of 1846–1847, p. 103, forbade teaching negroes.)

Constitution, 1865, Article IX. Section 2. Separate free public schools are required for white and negro children. The school fund must be appropriated in proportion to the number of children, without regard to color.

Constitution, 1865, Article I. Section 3. No person on account of color shall be subjected in law to any other restraints or disqualifications in regard to any personal rights than such as are laid upon others under like circumstances.

1866

General Statutes, 1866, p. 458. Section 2. All marriages between white persons and negroes are prohibited. Such marriages are absolutely void.

1868

Laws, 1868, p. 170. Separate school law repeated. (1869, Laws, p. 86 the same.)

1875

Constitution, Article VIII. Sections 2 et seq. All citizens are allowed the suffrage.

Constitution, Article XI. Section 3. Separate free public schools shall be established for the education of children of African descent.

1879

Revised Statutes, 1879. Section 1540. Persons having one-eighth or more negro blood are prohibited from marrying white persons. The penalty is two years in the penitentiary, or a fine not less than $100, or imprisonment in county jail not less than three months, or both fine and imprisonment. A jury may determine the amount of negro blood from appearance. Such marriages are void. (See Revised Statutes, 1845, p. 729, prohibiting intermarriage.)

1887

Laws, 1887, p. 264. A school for negro children shall be established in a district where there are more than fifteen children of required age. Where there are less than fifteen children, they may attend school in any district where a separate school is maintained for negro children. (See also Revised Statutes, 1909, Section 10,795, and Laws, 1909, p. 770.)

1889

Laws, 1889, p. 226. Separate free schools shall be established for the education of children of African descent; and it shall hereafter be unlawful in the public schools of this State for any colored child to attend any white school, or for any white child to attend a colored school.

1899

Revised Statutes, 1899. Sections 2919–2920. Descendants of colored persons dying intestate shall inherit, notwithstanding such descendants may have been slaves.

1909

Laws, 1909, p. 662. Marriages between white persons and negroes, or white persons and Mongolians are prohibited and absolutely void.

Laws, p. 599. A State Industrial Home for Negro Girls is instituted.

Montana

1871

Montana Territorial Laws, 1872, p. 627. Section 34. (Common School Law, 1871, Chapter 88, Section 34.) The education of children of African descent shall be provided for in separate schools. Upon the written application of parents or guardians of at least ten such children a separate school shall be established, and the education of a less number may be provided for by the trustees in separate schools in any other manner, and the same laws, rules, and regulations which apply to schools for white children shall apply to schools for colored children. (Law repeated in Laws, 1874, p. 129, Section 33, and Compiled Statutes of 1887, Section 1892.)

1889

Constitution, 1889, Article XI. Section 7. The public free schools of the State shall be open to all children and youths between the ages of six and twenty-one years.

1895

Montana C. and S., 1895. Section 1860. (Public School Law, 1895, Chapter 6, Article 8.) Every common school not otherwise provided for by law, shall be open to the admission of all children. (No mention whatever of separate schools, or of African children.)

1909

Laws, 49, p. 57. Section 1. Every marriage hereafter contracted between a white person and a negro or a person of negro blood, or in part negro, shall be utterly null and void.

Section 2. Same provision for a white person and Chinese.

Section 3. Same provision for a white person and Japanese.

Section 5. Any one solemnizing such a marriage is guilty of a misdemeanor; the penalty, a fine of $500, or imprisonment of one month, or both.

Nebraska

1857

Session Laws, 1857, p. 107, Chapter 33. Section 1. No Indian, negro, mulatto, or black person is allowed to give testimony in any cause.

1865

Session Laws, 1865, p. 109. The marriage of a white person with a negro or a mulatto is illegal and void. Misdemeanor, punishable by a fine of not more than $100, or imprisonment in the county jail not more than six months, or both. (Revised Statutes, 1866, p. 254.)

1866

Constitution, Article VII. Free white males only are allowed the franchise.

Revised Statutes, 1866, C. of C. P. Section 328. Every person of sufficient capacity to understand the obligation of an oath shall be competent to testify. Negroes and Indians who appear incapable of receiving just impressions of facts shall be incompetent to testify.

1867

Laws, 1867, p. 20. Strikes out "free white" from franchise requirements. No denial of elective franchise by reason of race or color.

1885

Laws, 1885, p. 393. (*Civil rights.*) All persons shall be entitled to full enjoyment of equal privileges of inns, public conveyances, barber shops, theaters, and other places of amusement, subject only to the conditions and limitations established by law, and applicable alike to every person.

The penalty for violation of above by denying except for reasons by law applicable to all persons the full enjoyment of the accommodations, advantages, facilities, enumerated in the foregoing, is that such persons shall be guilty of a misdemeanor, and shall be fined not less than $10, nor more than $25, and pay the costs of the prosecution.

1893

Laws, 1893, p. 141. Civil Rights Law of 1885 amended. Adds "restaurants" after "inns." The penalty is changed to a fine of from $25 to $100, and payment of costs.

1911

Statutes, 1911. Section 3196. Upon the dissolution or decree of nullity of a marriage prohibited on account of consanguinity or of any marriage between a white and a colored person, the issue of such marriage shall be deemed illegitimate.

Statutes, 1911. Section 4275. Marriages are void between a white person and one of one-quarter or more negro blood.

1913

Revised Statutes, 1913. Section 7893. Indians and negroes who appear to be incapable of receiving just impressions of facts respecting which they are examined, or of relating them intelligently and truly, shall be incompetent as witnesses.

Nevada

1861

Laws, 1861, p. 93. If any white man or woman intermarry with any black person, mulatto, Indian, or Chinese, it is a misdemeanor. The penalty is imprisonment in the State prison from one year to two years. Uniting such persons in marriage is a misdemeanor, punishable by imprisonment in the State prison from one to three years.

If any white person lives and cohabits with any black person, Indian, or Chinese in a state of fornication each shall be fined from $500 to $100 or confined in the county jail from one to six months, or both. Fines shall be set apart for the common school fund.

1864

Constitution, 1864, Article II. Section 1. White males only are allowed the vote.

1865

Laws, 1864–1865, p. 426. Section 50. Negroes, Mongolians, and Indians shall not be admitted into public schools. The superintendent of public instruction may withhold from a school district all share of State school funds in such case.

The Board of Trustees of any district may, if deemed advisable, establish a separate school for education of negroes, Mongolians, and Indians and use public school funds for the support of same.

Laws, 1864–1865, p. 403. Negroes have right to testify if not either in favor of or against a white person. The credibility of such negro, black, or mulatto person shall be left entirely with the jury.

1866

Revised Laws, 1866. Section 3128. No distinction shall be made in the construction or execution of these laws on account of race or color. (Homestead Laws.)

1873

Laws, 1873, p. 89. Act to compel children to attend school. All children from eight to fourteen years of age shall attend schools. (No separate district or separate schools mentioned.)

1912

Revised Laws, 1912. Section 6514–6517. It is unlawful for a person of Caucasian or white race to intermarry with any person of Ethiopian or black race, Malay or brown race, Mongolian or yellow race, or Indian or red race, within the State. Such person is guilty of a gross misdemeanor. The minister, etc., who performs the ceremony of marriage shall be guilty of a misdemeanor.

A white person who lives and cohabits with any black person, mulatto, Indian, or any person of Malay or brown, or Mongolian or yellow race, in a state of fornication, shall be fined not to exceed $500, nor less than $100, or confined in the county jail from six months to one year, or both.

New Hampshire

1694

May 24, 1694, 1 Province Laws, 570. The same measure and same text as Act of May 14, 1718, quoted, but the law was disallowed by the Queen, November 19, 1706, for certain reasons.

1714

May 15, 1714, Chapter 16. Laws, 1716 edition, p. 48; 1771 edition, p.52. An Act to Prevent Disorders in the Night. "Whereas Great Disorders Insolencies & Burglaries are oft times Raised & committed in the Night time by Indian, Negro, & Molatto, Servants and Slaves;

"Be it Enacted that Noe Indian, Negro, or Molatto, Servant or Slave may presume to be absent from the ffamilies where they Respectively belong or be found abroad in the Night time after

Nine a Clock; Unless it be upon Errand for their Respective Masters or Owners."

All officials and householders empowered to apprehend any such. Then to go to the House of Correction to receive the Discipline of the House, and then be dismissed back home; or where there is no House of Correction to be openly whipped not exceeding ten stripes.

1716

January 6, 1715–1716, Chapter 2. Laws, 1716 edition, p. 57; 1771 edition, p. 57. No Innholder, Taverner, etc., shall suffer any apprentice, servant, or Negro to sit drinking in the House or to have any manner of drink there without special order or allowance of their respective Masters, on pain of forfeiting the sum of ten shillings, for every such offence.

1718

May 14, 1718, Chapter 21. Laws, 1716 edition, p. 91; 1771 edition, p. 92. An Act for the Regulating of the Militia. Section 12. This act exempted from all military training certain state officials, ministers, elders, and deacons of churches, physicians, schoolmasters, etc., and Indians and negroes. Also disabled persons.

May 14, 1718, Chapter 25. Laws, 1716 edition, p. 99; 1771 edition, p. 101. Act for restraining inhuman severities.

The second section says: "If any Person shall wilfully kill his Indian or Negro Servant or Servants, he shall be Punished with Death."

1792

June, 1792. Repeal of law of 1714 to "Prevent Disorders in the Night."

June 20, 1792. Repeal of law of 1715–1716, January 6, as to negroes, etc., drinking in taverns.

June 20, 1792. Repeal of law of May 14, 1718, "Act for restraining inhuman severities."

1857

Laws, 1857, Chapter 1955. Section 1. African descent shall not disqualify a person from becoming a citizen of the State.

New Jersey

1702

Laws, 1702, p. 640. When negroes are vended in New Jersey, an account of them shall be transmitted.

Laws, 1702, p. 642. Negroes are to be converted and not murdered.

1844

Constitution, 1844, Article II. Section 1. White males only have the right of suffrage.

1853

Laws, 1853, p. 374. Section 3. When any poor colored servant has a right to support from any person, or estate of a deceased, such servant may be removed in same manner as other paupers to the township where he last served. Nothing herein contained shall be deemed to exonerate any person or estate from liability to support such poor colored servant, and the town may recover all charges for support.

1881

Laws, 1881, p. 186. No children between the age of five and eighteen years of age shall be excluded from any public school in the State on account of his or her religion, nationality, or color.

1884

Public Laws, p. 339. Section 1. All persons are entitled to equal rights and privileges of inns, public conveyances on land or water, theaters and other places of public amusement, subject only to conditions applicable alike to citizens of every race and color regardless of any previous condition of servitude.

Section 2. Persons violating this act or aiding or inciting thereto must forfeit and pay to person aggrieved $500, also are guilty of misdemeanor; punishable by a fine not less than $500 nor more than $1,000, or imprisonment of not less than thirty days nor more than one year.

Section 3. No citizen possessing other qualifications shall be disqualified for service as grand or petit juror in any court of the State on account of race, color, or previous condition of servitude. Anyone failing to summon or attempting to exclude any person because of race shall be guilty of a misdemeanor and be fined not more than $5,000.

1894

Public Laws, 1894, p. 537. Provides for the examination by the State Superintendent of public instruction of the records of the Colored Industrial Education Association of New Jersey.

Public Laws, 1894, p. 536. Provides for a manual training school for colored youth.

1895

Public Laws, 1895, p. 274. Militia. In addition to the force hereinbefore organized there shall be allowed four companies of colored infantry.

1898

Public Laws, 1898, p. 853. No cemetery association shall refuse to permit the burial of any deceased person therein because of the color of such deceased person. Any cemetery association offending is guilty of a misdemeanor.

1902

Public Laws, 1902, p. 441. No discrimination by insurance companies against persons wholly or partly of African descent is permitted.

Insurance discrimination is forbidden in standard form (nothing as to certificate). The section is applicable only to contracts of insurance issued on lives of persons resident in this State at time application for such insurance shall be made. Nothing shall require an agent or company to take or receive the application for insurance of any person or to issue a policy of insurance to any person.

Each violation of act to be punishable by a fine of $500 and costs. Half of penalty to be paid by Commissioner of Banking and Insurance to the local firemen's relief association, the other half to use of State.

1903

Public Laws, 1903 (Second Sp. Session), p. 48. No child between the age of four and twenty years shall be excluded from any public school on account of religion, nationality, or color. A member of any board of education who shall vote to exclude from any public school such child on account of religion, nationality, or color shall be guilty of a misdemeanor, and punished by fine of not less than $50 nor more than $250, or by imprisonment in county jail, workhouse, or penitentiary for not less than thirty days or more than six months, or by both.

Public Laws, 1903 (Second Sp. Session), p. 76. A normal training and industrial school for colored youth is provided for. It shall be hereafter conducted by the State Board of Education. Tuition shall be free.

New Mexico

1850

Organic Act, 1850. Section 6. Free white persons only are given the franchise.

1857

Laws, 1856–1857, p. 48. No free negroes shall come to this Territory for the purpose of establishing themselves here, for a time exceeding thirty days. Attempt so to do is punishable by from $50 to $100 fine and moreover by a sentence to hard labor in the penitentiary from one year to two years.

Section 2. If they refuse to leave after complying with terms of sentence, they shall have hard labor in penitentiary from two to four years.

Section 3. If any negro or mulatto shall marry or cohabit with any woman of the white race, he is liable to a penalty of hard labor in penitentiary from two to three years. This shall not affect free negroes or mulattoes married before Act.

Section 4. If any woman of the white race marry or cohabit with any free negro or mulatto, she is liable as in the preceding section. Any minister, etc., solemnizing the prohibited matrimonies is liable to from $100 to $200 fine.

Section 5. An owner setting free any negro must transport same beyond limits of territory within thirty days. From $100 to $500 fine for violation.

Section 6. A free negro or mulatto now residing in territory, must give bond for good conduct, or else be liable to penalties of Section 1.

1866

Laws, 1865–1866, p. 90. Act of January 29, 1857, concerning free negroes is hereby repealed. (Repeal includes section prohibiting intermarriage.)

1901

Laws, 1901, p. 147. Section 1. Any teachers, school directors, or members of any board of education connected with the common schools in this State who shall refuse to receive any pupil at a school on account of race or nationality, the said pupil being entitled to attend, shall be guilty of a misdemeanor, and punished by a fine from $50 to $100 and imprisonment in county jail for three months, and shall be forever barred from teaching school or from holding any office of honor or profit in this territory.

Section 2. The superintendent of the county is required summarily to remove from office or employment any person violating the provisions of previous section; upon his failure to do so he shall be removed from his office by the superintendent of public instruction, who is empowered to fill said vacancy.

1911

Constitution, 1911, Article VII. Section 3. Elective Franchise. The right of any citizen of the State to vote, hold office, or sit upon juries, shall never be restricted, abridged, or impaired on account of religion, race, language, or color, or inability to speak, read, or write the English or Spanish languages, except as may be otherwise provided in this Constitution; and the provisions of this Section and of Section 1 of this article shall never be amended except upon a vote of the people of this State in an election at which at least three-quarters of the electors voting in the whole State and at least two-thirds of those voting in each county of the State, shall vote for such amendment.

Constitution, 1911, Article XII. Section 1. Education. Free public schools open to all the children of school age in the State shall be established and maintained.

Section 10. Children of Spanish descent in the State of New Mexico shall never be denied the right and privilege of admission and attendance in the public schools or other public educational institutions of the State, and they shall never be classed in separate schools, but shall forever enjoy perfect equality with other children in all public schools and educational institutions of the State.

New York

1777

Constitution, 1777, Article VII. Every male inhabitant of full age, etc., is entitled to vote.

1813

Laws, 36th Session, p. 247. (*Van Ness & Woodworth.*) *Chapter 41, Section 8.* Voter to be freeholder, etc.

Section 11. Whenever any black or mulatto person shall present himself to vote, he shall produce a certificate of his freedom.

Section 12. Every black or mulatto residing in the state may make proof of his freedom before a judge, etc., and a written certificate shall be issued by the judge, etc.

1814

Laws, 37th Session, p. 84. A certificate of freedom shall be required to be produced at all elections in the city and county of New York, and without it no black or mulatto person shall be permitted to vote.

1814–1815

Laws, 1814–1815, p. 22. The Governor of the State is authorized to raise two regiments of free men of color, for the defense of State, for three years unless sooner discharged. Each regiment shall consist of 1,080 men. They shall be formed into a brigade. All commissioned officers of the regiments in the brigade shall be white men.

1821

Constitution, 1821, Article II. Section 1. The following are entitled to vote: "Every male citizen, an inhabitant of the State one year preceding any election, and shall have within the year next preceding the election paid a tax to the State or county, assessed upon his real or personal property; or shall by law be exempted from taxes, etc., and also every male citizen three years next preceding the election an inhabitant of the State, and shall have within the last year been assessed to labor upon public highways, or paid the equivalent; but no man of color, unless he shall have been for three years a citizen of this State, and for one year next preceding any election shall be seized and possessed of a freehold estate of the value of $250, over and above all debts and incumbrance charged thereon, shall be entitled to vote at any election. And no person of color shall be subject to direct taxation unless he shall be seized and possessed of such real estate as aforesaid."

1824

Laws, 1824, Chapter 177. No negro or mulatto shall vote in the councils of the Stockbridge Indians.

1833

Article II, Section 1 of Constitution. Amended by Amendment No. 11 in 1833, making it as appears in 1846 Constitution, given below.

1845

Laws, 1845, p. 327. The Mayor and common council of Brooklyn are authorized as they may deem expedient, to lay out school districts for colored children in City of Brooklyn. All provisions of law relating to common schools, etc., shall apply.

1846

Constitution, 1846, Article II. Section 1. Every male citizen, an inhabitant of the State for one year next preceding any election, shall be entitled to vote. But no man of color, unless three years a citizen of the State, and for one year next preceding the election possessed of a freehold estate of the value of $250 over and above all debts and encumbrances, and shall have been actually rated and paid a tax thereon, shall be entitled to vote, and no person of color shall be subject to direct taxation unless he shall be seized and possessed of such real estate as aforesaid.

1847

Laws, 1847, Volume II, p. 527. Incorporating the New York Society for the Promotion of Education among Colored Children. It may establish schools for colored children from four to sixteen years of age. The income of the society shall not exceed $10,000. The schools shall be under direction of the board of education of the city of New York but under the immediate government of the corporation. They shall participate in apportionment of school moneys from the school fund in like manner and to same extent as for schools of the public school society.

Laws, 1847, p. 714. Section 417. Separate colored schools may be established in any town or city of the state. They shall be under the charge of the school trustees of the school district. They shall divide the school money with the other schools in proportion to the number of respective pupils.

1852

Laws, 1852, p. 430. The people of the village of Canandaigua are authorized to establish a school for education of colored children of village exclusively. Provisions as to levying tax for same. The school under the control of the village trustees. No colored children shall be allowed to attend the school kept in any school district in Canandaigua except the colored school, without permission of all trustees of such school district.

1864

Laws, 1864, Chapter 555, p. 1211. An Act to consolidate the general acts relating to public institutions.

Title X, p. 1281. Schools for colored children. Section 1. School authorities of any city or village may, when deemed expedient, establish a separate school for the instruction of children of African descent of five to twenty-one years of age. It shall be supported in same manner and subject to same rules and regulations as white schools.

Section 3. Only legally qualified teachers shall be employed for such schools.

1868

Constitution, 1868, Article II. Section 1. Every male inhabitant of the state shall be entitled to vote, etc. (No reference to persons of color.)

1870

Laws, 1870. I, p. 922. (*Repeal of property qualification.*) Repeals all laws requiring of a colored man offering to vote any different oath from that required for a white man, or requiring different questions or answers.

It is not lawful for registers, or officers of election, to reject a name from registry, or the vote, of any colored man, except for causes making it their duty to reject the name or the vote of a white man. Penalty, a misdemeanor with a fine of $500 and six months' imprisonment.

1873

Laws, 1873, p. 303. No citizen of the State shall by reason of race, color, or previous condition of servitude be excepted or excluded from full and equal enjoyment of the accommodations furnished by innkeepers, by common carriers, whether on land or water, by licensed owners, managers or lessees of theaters, or other places of amusement, by trustees, commissioners, superintendents, teachers and other officers of common schools and public institutions of learning, and by cemetery associations.

Section 2. Violation is a misdemeanor, punishable by $50 to $500 fine.

Section 3. Discrimination against any citizen on account of color by the use of the word "white" or any other term in any law, statute, ordinance, or regulation now existing in this State is repealed and annulled.

1881

Laws, 1881, Chapter 400, p. 541. No person shall be denied full and equal enjoyment of accommodations, advantages, facilities, and privileges of all hotels, taverns, restaurants, public conveyances on land and water, theaters and other places of public resort or amusement, because of race, creed, or color. Denying because of race, creed, or color, or aiding or inciting thereto every offense is a misdemeanor and punished accordingly.

1891

Laws, 1891, Chapter 119, p. 288. No life insurance company doing business within this State shall make any distinction or discrimination between white persons and colored persons, wholly or partially of African descent, as to premiums or rates charged for policies upon lives, nor demand a greater premium from such colored persons than is at that time required from white persons of same age, sex, general condition of health and prospect of longevity; nor require any rebate or discount upon amount to be paid in case of death of such colored persons insured, nor insert in a policy any condition whereby such person insured shall bind himself or his heirs to accept any sum less than full value of policy, other than imposed on white persons in similar cases, and any such condition or stipulation shall be void. Violation is a misdemeanor, punishable by fine from $50 to $500.

1893

Laws, 1893, Volume 2, Chapter 692, p. 1720. An Act amending the penal code in a number of ways. Repeats both 1873 and 1881 Civil Rights laws, as Section 1 (1873) and Section 2 (1881). Penalty, $50 to $500 fine.

1894

Laws, 1894, p. 1288. (*Consol. School Law, p. 1811.*) *Article II. Schools for colored children. Same as 1864 law, in substance. Adds new paragraph. Section 31.* The colored schools in city of New York, now existing and in operation, shall be classed and continued as ward schools and primaries and shall be open for education of pupils for whom admission is sought, without regard to race or color.

Only qualified teachers shall be employed. No person shall be employed to teach any of such schools who shall not, at the time of such employment, be legally qualified.

1895

Laws, 1895, Vol. I, Chapter 1042, p. 974. (*Civil Rights Law, Article IV, Section 40*). *Section 1.* Equal rights in places of public accommodation or amusement. All persons shall be entitled to the full and equal accommodations, advantages, facilities and privileges of inns, restaurants, hotels, eating-houses, bath-houses, barber shops, theaters, music-halls, public conveyances on land and water, and all other places of public accommodation or amusement, subject only to conditions and limitations established by law and applicable alike to all citizens.

Section 2. (*Section 41*). Penalty for violation: Any person who shall violate any of the provisions except for reasons applicable alike to all citizens of every race, creed, or color, and regardless of race, creed, or color, by denying the full enjoyment of any of the accommodations, advantages, facilities, or privileges in said section enumerated, or by aiding such denial, shall for every such offense forfeit and pay not less than $100 nor more than $500 to the person aggrieved thereby, and shall also be deemed guilty of a misdemeanor, and upon conviction thereof shall be fined not less than $100 nor more than $500, or shall be imprisoned not less than thirty days nor more than ninety days, or both.

Section 3. No citizen of the State possessing all other qualifications, shall be disqualified to serve as grand or petit juror in any court on account of race, creed, or color. Any person charged with any duty in the selection or summoning of jurors, failing to summon any individual for the cause aforesaid, is guilty of a misdemeanor and may be fined $100 to $500, or imprisoned from thirty to ninety days, or both. (See Consol. Laws, 1909, Vol. I, p. 313.)

1899

Laws, 1899, Volume II, Chapter 724, p. 1556. Penal code amended by inserting Section 383a. Discrimination, when prohibited. If a person who owns, occupies, manages, or controls a building, park, enclosure, or other place, opens same to public generally at stated periods or otherwise, he shall not discriminate against any person or class of persons in the price charged for admission thereto. Violation of this act is a misdemeanor.

1900

Laws, 1900, Volume II, Chapter 492, p. 1173. An Act to secure equal rights to colored children in State of New York, and to repeal 1894, Chapter 556, Article II, Section 28.

Section 1. No person shall be refused admission into or be excluded from any public school in the State of New York on account of race or color.

Section 2. Repeals previous separation law of 1864.

1910

Education law (*Volume VIII of Consol. Laws, 1910*), *Article XXXVI, p. 200. Section 920.* No exclusion on account of race or color. No person shall be refused admission into or be excluded from any public school in the State of New York on account of race or color. (See 1900 Law.)

Section 921. Provisions for separate schools. The trustees of any union school district, or of any school district organized under a special act, may, when the inhabitants of any district shall so determine, by resolution, at any annual meeting, or at a special meeting called for that purpose, establish separate schools for instruction of colored children resident therein, and such school shall be supported in the same manner and receive the same care, and be furnished with same facilities for instruction, as the white schools therein. (See 1894 Law.)

1913

Laws, 1913, p. 1405. Authorized an Emancipation Proclamation Commission of nine members to arrange in the City of New York an exhibition and celebration to commemorate the fiftieth anniversary of the Emancipation Proclamation. Authorized a full exhibit to show the progress of the colored people since the Emancipation Proclamation. Appropriation of $25,000.

Laws, 1913, p. 2201. Section 1. Laws of 1909, Chapter 41, Article II, Military Law, Chapter 36 of Consolidated Laws, p. 2333, amended by adding new section, to be section 40.

Section 40. Colored Regiment of Infantry. Within three months after this section takes effect, the adjutant general shall organize and equip a colored regiment of infantry in the City of New York. Such regiment when organized and equipped shall become a part of the national guard of the State of New York, and subject to all the statutes, rules, and regulations governing such national guard. The officers of such regiment shall be commissioned by the governor subject to the provisions of this chapter in relation to eligibility and examination. The armory board of the City of New York shall provide quarters for such regiment.

(A different Section 40 was added by Laws, 1911, Chapter 285, p. 685, and amended by Laws, 1915, p. 1217. This different Section 40 relates to Aides.)

Laws, 1913, p. 481. Act to amend Civil Rights Law, Chapter 6 of Consolidated Laws (Laws, 1895, Vol. I, p. 974), to read as follows:

Section 1. Section 40 is amended to read as follows:

Section 40. All persons are entitled to the full and equal accommodations of any place of public accommodation, resort, or amusement, subject only to conditions and limitations established by law and applicable alike to all persons. No person, being the owner, lessee, proprietor, manager, superintendent, agent, or employee of any such place, shall directly or indirectly refuse, to any person, any of the accommodations thereof, or directly or indirectly publish, circulate, issue, display, post, or mail any written or printed communication, notice, or advertisement to the effect that any of the accommodations of any such place shall be refused to any person on account of race, creed, or color, or that the patronage or custom thereat of any person belonging to any particular race, creed, or color is unwelcome, objectionable, or not acceptable, desired, or solicited. The production of any such written or printed communication, notice, or advertisement purporting to relate to any such place and to be made by any person being the owner or manager thereof, shall be presumptive evidence in any civil or criminal action that the same was authorized by such person. A place of public accommodation, resort, or amusement shall be deemed to include any inn, tavern, or hotel, whether conducted for the entertainment of transient guests, or for the accommodation of those seeking health, recreation, or rest, any restaurant, eating house, public conveyance on land or water, bath house, barber shop, theater, and music hall. Nothing herein contained shall be construed to prohibit the mailing of a private communication in writing sent in response to a specific written inquiry.

Section 2. Section 41 is amended to read as follows:

Section 41. The penalty for violation, or aiding or inciting violation of any of said provisions, is a forfeit from $100 to $500, to be recovered by the person aggrieved or by any resident of this State to whom such person shall assign his cause of action; and the offender shall also be deemed guilty of a misdemeanor, punishable by a fine of $100 to $500, or imprisonment from thirty days to ninety days, or both.

1915

Laws, 1915, p. 2351. Historical and Industrial Exposition. The Governor was authorized to appoint five commissioners for the State of New York for the National Exposition at Richmond, Virginia, July and August, 1915, under the auspices of the National Historical and Industrial Association, to celebrate the fiftieth anniversary of Emancipation.

The commissioners were directed to gather an exhibit reflecting the thought and genius of the negroes of New York.

North Carolina

1866

Laws, 1866, Chapter 40. Section 5. Persons formerly slaves, who have complied with provisions of Act of March 10, 1866, are deemed lawfully married.

1868

Laws, 1868, p. 35. White and colored members of the detailed militia shall not be compelled to serve in same companies.

Constitution, 1868, Article VI. Section 1. Removed limitation of suffrage to white persons.

1873

Laws, 1873, p. 587. Marriages between a white person and a negro or Indian, or a white person and a person of negro or Indian descent to third generation inclusive, are void. No marriage followed by cohabitation and birth of issue shall be declared void after death of either of the parties for any of causes stated, except for that one of the parties was a white person and the other a negro or Indian, or of negro or Indian descent to third generation inclusive, and for bigamy. (See Laws, 1834, Chapter 24, and Laws, 1838, p. 33.)

1874

Laws, 1874–1875, p. 92. No white children shall be bound as apprentices to colored masters or mistresses.

1875

Constitution, 1875, Article IX. Section 3. Children of the white race and children of the colored race shall be taught in separate public schools, but there shall be no discrimination made in favor of, or to the prejudice of, either race.

Constitution, 1875, Article XIV. Section 8. All marriages between a white person and a negro or between a white person and a person of negro descent to third generation inclusive, are hereby forever prohibited.

1876–1877

Laws, 1876–1877, p. 438. The State Board of Education may establish normal schools for young men of the white race. It may also establish a normal school for young men of the colored race, to be teachers in the schools of the colored race. Students shall be expected to teach not less than three years after leaving school. A preparatory department may also be established.

1877

Laws, 1876–1877, p. 589. "WHEREAS, In the providence of God, the colored people have been set free, and this is their country and their home, as well as that of the white people, and there should be nothing to prevent the two races from dwelling together in the land in harmony and peace;

"WHEREAS, We recognize the duty of the stronger race to uphold the weaker, and that upon it rests the responsibility of an honest and faithful endeavor to raise the weaker race to the level of intelligent citizenship; and

"WHEREAS, The colored people have been erroneously taught that legislation under Democratic auspices would be inimical to their rights and interests, thereby causing a number of them to entertain honest fears in the premises,

"The General Assembly of North Carolina do resolve, That, while we regard with repugnance the absurd attempts, by means of 'Civil Rights' Bills, to eradicate certain race distinctions, implanted by nature and sustained by the habits of forty centuries; and while we are sure that good government demands for both races alike that the great representative and executive offices of the country should be administered by men of the highest intelligence and best experience in public affairs, we do, nevertheless, heartily accord alike to every citizen, without distinction of race or color, equality before the law.

"RESOLVED, That we recognize the full purport and intent of that amendment to the Constitution of the United States which confers the right of suffrage and citizenship upon the people of color, and that part of the Constitution of North Carolina conferring educational privileges upon both races: that we are disposed and determined to carry out in good faith these as all other constitutional provisions."

1879

Laws, 1879, Chapter 73. Children of colored parents born before January 1, 1868, of persons living together as man and wife, are declared legitimate children of the parents or either one of them.

1885

Laws, 1885, Chapter 51. Section 2. p. 92. The persons residing in Robeson and Richmond counties, supposed to be descendants of a friendly tribe once residing in eastern portion of State, known as Croatan Indians, shall be known and designated as Croatan Indians. They and their descendants shall have separate schools for their children and there shall be excluded from such separate schools for the Croatan Indians all children of the negro race to the fourth generation.

1887

Public Laws, 1887, p. 499. (Amending the provision that all marriages between an Indian and a negro shall be void.) Amended by adding "Provided this act shall only be applicable to the Croatan Indians."

1889

Laws, 1889, Chapter 169. Section 17. No white child shall be bound to any other than a white person, and no negro child shall be bound to any white person, if a competent and suitable negro can be found in the county who desires such child bound to him.

1899

Laws, 1899, Chapter 384, p. 539. All railroad companies and steamboat companies engaged as common carriers, other than street railways, shall provide separate but equal accommodations for the white and colored races on all passenger trains and steamboats carrying passengers. Such accommodations may be furnished by railroad companies either by separate passenger cars or by compartments in passenger cars, which shall be provided by the railroads under the supervision and direction of the Board of Railroad Commissioners. These requirements shall not apply to relief trains in cases of accident, to Pullman or sleeping cars or through express trains that do not stop at all stations and are not used ordinarily for travelling from station to station, to negro servants in attendance on their employers, to officers or guards transporting prisoners, or to prisoners so transported.

Section 2. The railroad commissioners are authorized to exempt branch lines and narrow guaged railroads, if in their judgment enforcement of this act is unnecessary to secure the comfort of passengers, by reason of light passenger traffic or small number of colored passenger travellers on such narrow guaged or branch lines.

Section 3. When a car or a compartment of a car for either race is completely filled at a station where no extra car can be had, and the increased number of passengers could not be foreseen, the conductor is authorized to assign a portion of the car or of the compartment for one race to passengers of the other race.

Section 4. All railroad companies shall furnish first and second class passenger accommodations.

Section 5. A company failing to comply with this act shall be fined $100 per day, each day to be a separate offense, to be recovered in action brought by any passenger on any train or steamboat who has been furnished accommodations only in a car or compartment with a person of a different race, in violation of the provisions of this act.

1901

Public Laws, 1901, p. 64. In determining the right of any child to attend the schools of either race, the rule laid down in Section 1810 of the Code, regulating marriages, shall be followed. (Provision of Constitution of 1875, XIV, 8.)

Public Laws, 1901, p. 351. Amendment to Law of 1899. Struck out word "passenger," in passenger trains, etc., making it read "all trains and steamboats carrying passengers." Inserted in Section 2, after "railroads" "and mixed trains carrying both freight and passengers." Added at end of the sentence, "and mixed passengers."

1903

Laws, 1903, p. 756. Section 22. All white children shall be taught in schools for the white race (and vice versa), but no child with negro blood in its veins, however remote the strain, shall attend a school for the white race, and no such child shall be considered a white child.

1907

Public Laws, 1907, p. 1238. All street, interurban, and suburban railway companies shall set apart so much of the front portion of each car as necessary for occupation by white passengers, and so much of the rear portion as necessary for occupation by colored passengers, and shall require as far as practicable the white and colored passengers each to occupy the respective part of car so set aside.

Section 2. Any white person entering a street car to become a passenger shall, if necessary to carry out the purposes of this act, occupy the first vacant seat in the aisle nearest the front of the car, and a colored person the first vacant seat nearest the rear end of said car. Provided, no contiguous seats on the same bench shall be occupied by the white and colored passengers at the same time unless or until all other seats are occupied.

Section 5. Any officer violating Section 1 is guilty of a misdemeanor and may be fined or imprisoned in the discretion of the court.

Section 6. Any person violating Section 2 is guilty of a misdemeanor and may be fined not more than $50 or imprisoned not more than thirty days. He may be ejected by the conductor or other agents charged with operation of the car, who are hereby invested with police powers to carry out the provisions of this act.

Section 7. This act shall not apply to colored nurses of white children, while in attendance upon such children then in their charge, or to a colored attendant in charge of a sick or infirm white person.

Section 8. Such companies shall not be liable for a mistake in the designation of any passenger to a seat set apart for the other race.

1908

Revisal, 1908. Section 4086. Children of the white race and children of the colored race shall be taught in separate public schools, but there shall be no discrimination in favor of either race. All white children shall be taught in the public schools provided for the white race, and all colored children shall be taught in the public schools provided for the colored race, but no child with negro blood in his veins, however remote the strain, shall attend a school for the white race; and no such child shall be considered a white child. The descendants of the Croatan Indians shall have separate schools for their children.

1909

Public Laws, 1909, p. 1215. White and colored persons shall not be confined and shackled together in the same room of any building or tent either in the state penitentiary or at any state or county convict camp during eating or sleeping hours, and at all other times separation of the two races shall be as complete as practicable. Any officer violating the above provision shall be guilty of misdemeanor and fined not more than $50 or imprisoned not more than thirty days.

Public Laws, 1909, p. 1256. Amending Public Laws, 1907, Chapter 850. The act strikes out all of Section 7 after the word "to" in line one, and adds the words: "Nurses or attendants of children or of sick or of infirm of a different race, while in attendance upon such children, sick, or infirm persons."

1911

Public Laws, 1911, p. 286. A Reform and Manual Training School for Colored Youths is authorized for the training and the moral and industrial development of the criminally delinquent colored children of the State under sixteen years of age.

1915

Public Laws, 1915, p. 355. In every public and private hospital, sanatorium, and institution in North Carolina where colored patients are admitted for treatment and where nurses are employed, it shall be mandatory upon the management of every such hospital, sanatorium, and institution to employ colored nurses to care for and wait upon said colored patients.

Section 2. Every person, firm, or corporation violating the provisions of this act is guilty of a misdemeanor, and upon conviction shall be fined $50 for each and every offense.

North Dakota

1867–1868

Laws of Dakota Territory, 1867–1868, p. 255. The word "white" was removed from the qualifications for suffrage.

Ohio

1804

Acts, 1803–1804, p. 63. An act to regulate black and mulatto persons.

No black or mulatto person is permitted to reside in the state without a certificate of his freedom. He must register in the county clerk's office. An employer cannot hire any blacks or mulattoes unless they have a certificate from the county clerk.

1806–1807

Laws, 1806–1807, p. 53. Section 1. A negro or mulatto is not permitted to settle in the State without filing bond for good behavior.

Section 4. No black or mulatto is to give evidence where either party to the cause is a white person.

1829

Laws, 1829, p. 72. Act to provide for the support and better regulation of common schools.

Section 1. A fund shall hereafter be raised for the use of common schools, for the instruction of youth of every class and grade without distinction, in reading, writing, arithmetic and other necessary branches of a common education. Provided that nothing in this act contained shall be so construed as to permit black or mulatto persons to attend the schools hereby established, or to compel them to pay any tax for support of such schools; but all taxes assessed on their property, for school purposes, shall be appropriated as the trustees of the several townships may direct, for the education of said black and mulatto persons therein, and for no other purpose, whatever.

1834

Laws, 1834, p. 22. Provisions as to recording certificates of color.

1837

Laws, 1837–1838, p. 21. (*School Act.*) A fund shall be provided for the education of all white youth in this state.

Section 2. In the tax levied on taxable property, the property of black and mulatto persons is excepted.

1838–1839

Laws, 1838–1839, p. 61. (*School Act.*) All white youth over four and under twenty-four years of age shall have equal privileges in all common schools in the state.

1847–1848

Laws, 1847–1848, p. 81. An act to provide for the establishment of common schools for the education of children of black and mulatto persons. Property of black and colored persons shall be taxed for schools for black or colored persons; but in any district in which the children of black and colored persons are permitted to attend the common schools with the children of white persons, then such fund is to be added to the common school fund of district.

Section 2. In a district with twenty black or colored children, it is lawful for colored persons to organize a district, to appoint school directors of their own number, and to erect a schoolhouse, etc.

Section 5. Where less than twenty black or colored children are desirous of attending school, the school directors shall admit said children into schools for white children, provided no written objection be filed with the directors.

Section 6. If the white inhabitants will not permit them to attend the schools for white children, no black or colored person's property shall be taxed for school purposes.

Section 9. Property of white persons shall not be taxed for schools for black or colored children contrary to the wishes of such tax-payers.

1848–1849

Laws, 1848–1849, p. 17. An act to authorize establishment of separate schools for education of colored children.

Section 1. The trustees of townships, etc., in case they shall not deem it expedient to admit the colored children into the regular common schools, are authorized and required to create school districts for colored persons.

Section 2. They shall call a meeting of colored tax-payers to organize for school purposes.

Section 6. Repeals Act of February 24, 1848 (Laws, 1847–1848, p. 81), for black schools, and Act of January 5, 1804 (Acts, 1803–1804, p. 63), to regulate black and mulatto persons, and acts amending the same of January 5, 1807 (Laws, 1806–1807, p. 53), and February 27, 1834 (Laws, 1834, p. 21).

1851

Constitution, 1851, Article V. Section 1. White males only are allowed the franchise.

1852

Laws, 1852, p. 429. (Act to provide for reorganization of common schools), p. 441. Township boards of education in the state are required to establish separate schools for colored children where more than thirty wish to attend school. Such schools shall be under control and management of the board of education. Division of funds shall be made according to the number of children, regardless of color.

1861

Laws, 1861, p. 6. Same as Laws, 1877, p. 277, statute against intermarriage, except adding in each section "guilty of misdemeanor, and." (Original law.)

1877

Laws, 1877, p. 277. (*See Laws, 1861.*) *Section 1.* A person of pure white blood, who intermarries, or has illicit carnal intercourse, with any negro or person having a distinct and visible admixture of African blood, and any negro, or person having a distinct and visible admixture of African blood, who intermarries, or has illicit carnal intercourse with any person of pure white blood, shall be fined not more than $100, or imprisoned not more than three months, or both.

Section 2. A probate judge who knowingly issues a license for the solemnizing of any marriage made penal by this act is guilty of a misdemeanor; and every person who knowingly solemnizes any such marriage shall be fined not more than $100 or imprisoned not more than three months, or both.

1878

Laws, 1878, p. 513. Section 50. Each board of education shall establish schools for free education of youth of school age—and where in their judgment it may be for the advantage of the district to do so, they may organize separate schools for colored children.

1881

Revised Statutes, 1881. Section 7032a. A Sabbath desecration provision prohibiting theatrical or other performances gives a long list including "Negro Minstrelsy."

1884

Laws, 1884, p. 15. Whereas it is essential to just government that we recognize and protect all men as equal before the law, and that a democratic form of government should mete out equal and exact justice to all, of whatever nativity, race, color, persuasion, religion or politics; and it being the appropriate object of legislation to enact great fundamental principles into law, therefore.

Section 1. Be it enacted by the General Assembly that all persons shall be entitled to the full and equal enjoyment of accommodations, facilities and privilege of inns, public conveyances on land and water, theaters and other places of public amusement, subject only to conditions and limitations established by law, and applicable alike to citizens of every race and color.

Section 2. For violating this act, or aiding or inciting thereto, there shall be a forfeit for each offense not to exceed $100 paid to the person aggrieved; also each offense shall be a misdemeanor, punishable by a fine of not less than $100 or imprisonment not less than thirty days, or both. Judgment in favor of the party aggrieved, or punishment upon an indictment, shall be a bar to either prosecution respectively.

Section 3. No citizen possessing all other qualifications prescribed by law shall be disqualified to serve as grand or petit juror in any court of the state on account of race or color; and any officer selecting jurors who shall exclude or fail to summon any citizen for the cause aforesaid, is guilty of a misdemeanor, punishable by a fine of not less than $100 or imprisonment not less than thirty days, or both.

Laws, 1884, p. 90. Section 1 of Act of 1884, p. 15, to protect all citizens in their civil and legal rights, is amended as follows:

Section 1. That all persons within the jurisdiction of said state shall be entitled to the full and equal enjoyment of the accommodations and privileges of inns, restaurants, eating-houses, barbershops, public conveyances on land or water, theaters, and all other places of public accommodation and amusement, subject only to the conditions and limitations established by law, and applicable alike to all citizens.

1887

Laws, 1887, p. 34. Sections 4008 (Separate school law of 1878, p. 513) and 6987 (Intermarriage law of 1877, p. 277, Section 1) and 6988 (Intermarriage law of 1877, p. 277, Section 2) of the Revised Statutes of Ohio are hereby repealed.

1889

Laws, 1889, p. 163. No life insurance company shall make any distinction or discrimination between white persons and colored persons wholly or partially of African descent, as to premiums or rates charged for policies upon the lives of such persons, nor shall any such company demand or require greater premiums from such colored persons than are at that time required by such company from white persons of the same age, etc., nor shall any such company make any rebate, diminution or discount upon the sum to be paid on such policy in case of the death of any colored person insured, nor insert in a policy any condition, nor make any stipulation whereby such person insured shall bind himself or his heirs to accept any sum less than the full value or amount of such policy, other than such as are imposed upon white persons in similar cases, and any such stipulation or condition so made or inserted shall be void.

Section 2. Any such company refusing an application of a colored person for insurance upon life shall furnish a certificate of a regular examining physician of the company stating that such person's application has been refused, not because such person is a person of color, but solely on such grounds of the general health and hope of longevity of such person as would be applicable to white persons of the same age and sex. Any corporation or any officer or agent of any corporation violating the provisions of this act shall be fined from $100 to $200.

Section 3. Nothing in this act shall be so construed as to require any agent or company to take or receive the application for insurance of any person.

1893

Laws, 1893, p. 345. Discrimination between insurants of same class, etc., in premiums, benefits, or terms of contract, shall be punished by a fine of not less than $100 nor more than $500, or imprisonment not more than thirty days, or both.

1894

Laws, 1894, p. 17. Amending act of 1884 (February 7 and March 27, Laws, 1884, p. 15, and p. 90) to read as follows:

Section 2. Any person violating the provisions of the foregoing section by denying to any citizen, except for reasons applicable alike to all citizens of every race and color, and regardless of color or race, the full enjoyment of any of the accommodations enumerated, or by aiding or inciting such denial, for every offense shall forfeit to the person aggrieved from $50 to $500 to be recovered in any court of competent jurisdiction in the county where said offense was committed, and shall also for every offense be found guilty of misdemeanor and fined from $50 to $500, or imprisoned from thirty to ninety days, or both, but one penalty shall be a bar to the other.

Section 3. No citizen possessing other qualifications shall be disqualified to serve as grand or petit juror in any court on account of race or color, and any officer, excluding or failing to summon any citizen for the cause aforesaid, is guilty of a misdemeanor punishable by a fine of from $50 to $500, or imprisonment from thirty to ninety days, or both.

Oklahoma

1890

Statutes, 1890, Article XIII. Section 6464. An act establishing a system of public schools in the Territory of Oklahoma.

Article 13. Separate schools. Separate schools may be established as follows. Each three years on the first Tuesday of April an election by school electors shall be held to vote for or against separate schools for white and colored children.

1897

Laws, 1897, p. 37. A Colored Agricultural and Normal University is authorized, for the instruction of male and female colored persons in the art of teaching.

Laws, 1897, p. 266. (School Law.) Article 1. Separate schools.

Section 1. Wherever there are eight colored children, there shall be a district formed. Where white children are in the minority there shall be separate schools for them. The taxes shall be prorated according to the number of children.

Section 9. Hereafter it shall be unlawful for any white child to attend a school for colored children (or vice versa). (See also Laws, 1901, p. 205, containing the same provision.)

1907

Constitution, 1907, Article 13. Section 3. Separate schools for white and colored children with like accommodation shall be provided by the legislature and impartially maintained.

Constitution, 1907, Article XXIII. Section 11. Wherever in the Constitution and laws of the state, the words "color" or "colored race," "negro" or "negro race" are used, they shall be construed to mean or apply to all persons of African descent. The term white race shall include all other persons.

Laws, 1907–1908, p. 201. Every railway company, urban or suburban car company, street car or interurban car railway company, etc., shall provide separate coaches or compartments for the accommodation of the white and the negro races, equal in all points of comfort and convenience.

Section 2. Every railroad company, street car company, urban or suburban or interurban car company shall provide for and maintain separate and equal waiting rooms at all passenger depots for the accommodation of the white and the negro races. Each waiting room shall have in a conspicuous place words in plain letters indicating the race for which it is set apart. It is unlawful to use or remain in any waiting room, toilet room, or use any water tank, in any passenger depot, set apart to a race to which one does not belong.

Section 3. The term negro includes every person of African descent.

Section 4. Each compartment of a railway coach divided by a good and substantial wooden partition with a door therein is deemed a separate coach. It shall bear in a conspicuous place appropriate words indicating the race intended for, and each compartment of an urban or suburban car company, interurban car or railway company, divided by a board or marker, in a conspicuous place, bearing words in plain letters, indicating the race intended for, shall be sufficient as a separate compartment.

Section 5. Violation of this act by any railway company, etc., is punishable by a fine of from $100 to $1,000. Each trip shall constitute a separate offense.

Section 6. Violation of this act by a passenger is a misdemeanor, punishable by a fine of from $5 to $25. If a passenger refuses to occupy the proper place the company may refuse to carry him.

Section 7. This act shall not apply to peace officers having in custody any person, or employees upon cars in discharge of duty, or freight trains carrying passengers in the caboose. Nothing shall prevent railway companies from hauling sleeping cars, dining or chair cars to be used exclusively by either white or negro passengers separately but not jointly.

Section 8. This act shall be posted in a conspicuous place in each passenger depot and in each passenger coach.

Section 9. This act shall not prevent the running of extra or special trains or cars, for the exclusive accommodation of either white or colored passengers.

Section 10. Conductors of trains, street cars, urban, suburban, or interurban lines, have authority to refuse a person admittance to a compartment in which he is not entitled to ride, and power to remove a passenger not entitled to ride. The refusal of the conductor to enforce separation is a misdemeanor, with $50 to $500 fine.

Section 11. The fines shall go to the common school fund.

Laws, 1907–1908, p. 556. The marriage of any person of African descent as defined by the Constitution of this state, to any person not of African descent, shall be unlawful and is hereby prohibited within this state.

Section 2. Violation of this provision is a felony punishable by a fine of not more than $500 and imprisonment from one to five years in the penitentiary.

Laws, 1907–1908, p. 694. Section 1. The public schools of the state of Oklahoma shall be organized and mantained upon a complete plan of separation between the white and colored races with impartial facilities for both races.

Section 2. The term "colored" as used in the first section shall be construed to mean all persons of African descent, who possess any quantum of negro blood, and the term "white" shall include all other persons. The term "public school" within the meaning of this act, shall include all schools provided for or maintained in whole or in part at public expense.

Section 3. That wherever there shall be established and maintained a separate school, a separate board of school officers shall be elected and chosen for the management of such school as is provided for by law for the election of other school officers. In districts having separate school buildings, the electors of each separate race shall meet as now provided by law at their respective schools for which said directors are to be elected and the electors of one race shall not participate in any election pertaining to the schools of the other race.

Section 4. Any teacher in this state who shall willingly and knowingly allow any child of the colored race to attend a school maintained for the white race, or allow any white child to attend a school maintained for the colored race, shall be deemed guilty of a misdemeanor, and upon conviction thereof shall be fined in any sum not less than $10 nor more than $50, and his certificate shall be cancelled and he shall not have another issued to him for a period of one year.

Section 5. It shall be unlawful for any person, corporation or association of persons to maintain or operate any college, school, or institution in this state where persons of the white and colored races are both received as pupils for instruction, and any person or corporation who shall operate or maintain any such college, school, or institution in violation hereof, shall be deemed guilty of a misdemeanor, and upon conviction thereof, shall be fined not less than $100 nor more than $500, and each day such school, college, or institution shall be open and maintained, shall be deemed a separate offense.

Section 6. That any instructor who shall teach in any school, college, or institution, where members of the white race and colored race are received and enrolled as pupils for instruction, shall be deemed guilty of a misdemeanor, and upon conviction thereof, shall be fined in any sum not less than $10 nor more than $50 for each offense, and each day any instructor shall continue to teach in any college, school, or institution shall be considered a separate offense.

Section 7. It shall be unlawful for any white person to attend any school, college, or institution where colored persons are received as pupils for instruction; and any one so offending shall be fined not less than $5 nor more than $20 for each offense, and each day such a person so offends as herein provided, shall be deemed a distinct and separate offense, provided that nothing in this act shall be so construed as to prevent any private school, college, or institution of learning from maintaining a separate or distinct branch thereof in a different locality.

1910

Laws, 1910, p. 208. Boards of county commissioners are authorized to sell real estate held for the purpose of separate or colored schools, where the same was not used.

1911

Laws, 1911, p. 262. Amending 1907–1908, Chapter 15, Article I, Section 7 (Laws, 1907–1908, p. 201, Section 7), to read as follows:

"And provided further that the Corporation Commission shall have power and authority to except any station or depot from the requirements of the act for such period of time as may be ordered, in any city or town where no negroes reside."

Oregon

1850–1851

Laws, 1850–1851, p. 181. (1849, September 26). No negro or mulatto shall come into the territory. If any such come on vessels, the owner or master of the vessel shall be responsible for his conduct and for his removing. The negro cannot leave the port of the vessel without the written permission of the master or owner.

1854

Laws, 1855, p. 551. The above law was repealed.

1855

Laws, 1855, p. 130. No negro, mulatto, or Indian shall be allowed to testify in an action to which a white person is a party.

1857

Constitution, 1857, Article I. Section 35. No free negro or mulatto, not residing in state, shall come, reside, or be within this state, or hold any real estate, or make any contracts, or maintain any suit therein; and legislative assemblies shall provide by penal laws for his removal and effectual exclusion, and for the punishment of persons bringing, or employing, or harboring him. (Not formally repealed. Abrogated by Fourteenth Amendment.)

Constitution, 1857, Article II. Section 6. No negro, Chinaman, or mulatto shall have the right of suffrage.

1862

Laws, 1862, p. 76. An annual poll tax of $5 is required from every negro, Chinaman, kanaka, or mulatto. If he fails to pay, he may be arrested and made to work on public highway.

Laws, 1862, p. 86. Marriage is prohibited when either party is a white person and the other a negro or a person of one-quarter or more of negro blood, and is absolutely void.

1867

Laws, 1867, p. 10. Section 1. (*Lord's Oregon Laws, 1910, p. 945. Section 2163.*) Hereafter it shall not be lawful for any white person to intermarry with any negro, Chinese, or any person having one-quarter or more negro, Chinese, or kanaka blood, or any person having more than one-half Indian blood. Such a marriage shall be absolutely null and void.

Section 2. The penalty for such intermarriage shall be imprisonment in the penitentiary or in the county jail for not less than three months nor more than one year.

Section 3. The penalty for licensing, or for performing the ceremony, for such a marriage, is imprisonment in the penitentiary or in the county jail for not less than three months nor more than one year, and a fine of not less than $100 nor more than $1,000.

1868

Laws, 1868, p. 18. It is lawful for every white male citizen of the age of sixteen years to keep and carry arms.

1872

Statutes, 1872. Section 700. All persons who can perceive and make known their perceptions to others are given the right to testify.

Pennsylvania

1838

Constitution, 1838, Article II. Section 1. White freemen are entitled to vote.

1854

Laws, 1854, Approved May 8. Directors are required to establish within their respective districts separate schools for the tuition of negro and mulatto children, wherever there are twenty or more pupils; and wherever such separate schools shall be established and kept open four months in any year, the directors shall not be compelled to admit such pupils into any other schools of the district. Schools in cities or boroughs shall be provided for out of the general funds for educational purposes. (Repealed in 1881.)

1867

Laws, 1867, March 22, p. 38. Section 1. Any railroad or railway corporation that shall exclude any person on account of color or race, or that shall refuse to carry in any of their cars, set apart for passengers, any person or persons on account of race or color, or that shall for such reason, compel or attempt to compel any person or persons, to occupy any particular part of their cars, set apart for the accommodation of people as passengers, shall be liable, in an action of debt, to the person thereby injured or aggrieved, in the sum of $500; the same to be recovered in an action of debt, as like amounts are now by law recoverable.

Section 2. Any agent or employee of any railroad who shall exclude, or allow to be excluded from any passenger cars, any person on account of color or race, or who shall refuse to carry such person on account of color or race, or who shall throw any car from the track, thereby preventing persons from riding, shall be deemed guilty of a misdemeanor, and upon conviction shall pay a fine not exceeding $500 nor less than $100, or be imprisoned for a term not exceeding three months, nor less than thirty days, or both.

1869

Laws, 1869, p. 160. Persons of color shall not be admitted to the subdistrict schools of Pittsburgh. (Repealed in 1872.)

1870

Laws, 1870, p. 53. Section 10. Every act providing that only white freemen are entitled to vote, is hereby repealed. Hereafter all freemen, without distinction of color, shall be enrolled and registered, and shall when otherwise qualified vote at all elections.

1872

Laws, 1872, p. 1,048. Repealed law of 1869, p. 160, as to schools in Pittsburgh.

1881

Laws, 1881, p. 76. Section 1. It shall be unlawful for any school director, superintendent, or teacher to make any distinction whatever, on account of or by reason of the race or color of any pupil or scholar who may be in attendance upon, or seeking admission to, any public or common school, maintained wholly or in part under the school laws of this commonwealth. (Repealed law of 1854.)

1887

Laws, 1887, p. 130. Civil Rights Bill. Any person, or corporation, being the owner or manager of any restaurant, hotel, railroad, street-railway, omnibus line, theater, concert hall, or place of entertainment or amusement, who shall refuse to accommodate, convey, or admit any person on account of race or color, over their lines, or into their hotel, or restaurant, theater, concert-hall, or place of amusement, shall upon conviction thereof be guilty of a misdemeanor, and be punished by a fine of not less than $50 and not more than $100.

Rhode Island

1798

Revised Laws, 1798, 1822, 1852, 1857. Intermarriage forbidden.

The marriage of a white person with a negro, Indian, or mulatto is absolutely null and void. Any person joining them in marriage is subject to a penalty of $200.

1872

Code, 1872, p. 325. Section 6. Prohibition of intermarriage. Penalty not over six months' imprisonment or $1,000 fine.

1881

Acts, 1881, p. 108. Repeal of the prohibition of intermarriage.

1882

General Laws, 1882, p. 155. No exclusion from school on account of race or color shall be allowed.

1885

Laws, 1884–1885, p. 171. No person shall be debarred from the full and equal enjoyment of the accommodations, advantages, facilities, and privileges of any licensed inns, public conveyances on land or water, or from any licensed places of public amusement, on account of race, color, or previous condition of servitude. Violation of this act shall be punished by a fine not exceeding $100. No citizen shall be disqualified for service as grand or petit juror in any court on account of race, color, or previous condition of servitude; and any officer who shall fail to select or summon any citizen for any of the causes aforesaid shall on conviction be fined not exceeding $100.

South Carolina

1865

Acts, 1864–1865, p. 291. Section 8. Marriage between a white person and a person of color shall be illegal and void.

Laws, 1865, p. 275. Persons of color constitute no part of the militia of the state.

Laws, 1865, p. 286. Negroes can testify in cases to which a person of color was a party.

1866

Acts, 1866, p. 393. An act to declare the rights of persons lately known as Slaves and Free Persons of Color. "Nothing herein shall be construed to repeal so much of the eighth section of the act ratified December 21, 1865, as enacts that "Marriage between a white person and a person of color shall be illegal and void."

1868

Constitution, 1868, Article X, Section 10. All the public schools, colleges and universities of the state, supported in whole or in part by the public funds, shall be free and open to all the children and youths of the state, without regard to race or color.

Constitution, 1868, Article I. Section 39. Distinction on account of race or color in any case whatever, shall be prohibited, and all classes of citizens shall enjoy equally all common, public, legal, and political privileges. (This included marriage, and rendered intermarriage lawful. See below, Laws, 1879, p. 3.)

1869

Laws, 1869–1870, p. 279. It is not lawful for common carriers, or any party engaged in business for which a license is required by law, to discriminate on account of race or color, or previous condition. The penalty is a fine of $1,000 and also hard labor in the penitentiary for five years. If the fine is not paid, then imprisonment in the penitentiary at hard labor for not less than six years.

The manager of a theater or place of amusement or recreation, if licensed or under any public rule, making discrimination, or refusing equal accommodation, on account of race, color or previous condition, is liable to $1,000 fine and imprisonment in the penitentiary for three years at hard labor.

Such person shall never vote or hold any office.

Every corporation or party holding any charter or license, violating this act, shall forfeit the charter or license. If having forfeited it, they continue to operate under the same, a penalty is imposed of a fine of $1,000 and inprisonment in the penitentiary for three years.

When charged with refusal to admit any person on account of race, color or previous condition, and the applicant is a colored or black person, the burden shall be on the defendant to show the same was not done in violation of this act.

Solicitors of the state are specially charged vigorously to enforce this act. Failure to do so is a misfeasance in office, and such solicitor shall forfeit his office, be incapable of holding office for five years, and be fined $500. No solicitor nor the attorney general shall settle or enter a nol. pros. in cases under this act without consent of court.

1870

Laws, 1870, p. 338. Wherever authority has heretofore been conferred by law upon any free white person to institute any suit or proceedings, or to prefer any information or complaint in any matter, civil, penal, or criminal, the same rights shall be enjoyed by, and the same remedies applicable to, all persons whatsoever, regardless of race or color, subject to the same conditions, and to none others.

1872

Laws, 1872, p. 183. All persons who, previous to their emancipation, occupied the relation of husband and wife and who are cohabiting as such, or who recognize the relation as still existing, shall be deemed husband and wife. The children of such marriages shall be deemed legitimate.

Laws, 1871–1872, pp. 162–163. Children of white fathers and negro mothers may inherit from the father if he did not marry another woman but continued to live with their mother.

1873

Revised Statutes, 1873. No mention of separate schools or the reverse.

1879

Laws, 1879, p. 3. Marriage between a white person and an Indian, negro, mulatto, mestizo, or half-breed shall be null and void, and of none effect.

Such marriage is a misdemeanor, subject to punishment of a fine of not less than $500, or imprisonment for not less than twelve months, or both.

Uniting persons of different race in bonds of matrimony, by a minister, magistrate, etc., is a misdemeanor, subject to the same penalty. (Reenacted intermarriage prohibition, which was repealed in 1868.) (Code, 1912, Section 3757.)

Kennington v. Catoe, 68 South Carolina, pp. 470, 475. Colored children, born after emancipation, of a free colored woman, who was married to a white man before the act of 1879 prohibiting intermarrying of races, can take property under a will as legitimate children. The decision held that before the Statute of 1879 there was no law in the state making illegal the marriage of a white man to a colored woman. (See also 76 N. C. 242, and 76 N. C. 251, for similar statements of the S. C. law.)

1895

Constitution, 1895, Article III. Section 33. The marriage of a white person with a negro or mulatto, or a person who shall have one-eighth or more of negro blood, is unlawful and void.

Constitution, 1895, Article XI. Section 8. Separate schools shall be provided for children of the white and the colored race, and no children of either race shall ever be permitted to attend a school provided for children of the other race.

1896

Laws, 1896, p. 171. Section 58. It shall be unlawful for pupils of one race to attend schools provided by boards of trustees for persons of another race.

Laws, 1896, p. 174. The establishment is authorized of the Colored Normal Industrial and Mechanical College of the South Carolina Branch of South Carolina University for the higher education of colored youth of state.

1898

Laws, 1898, p. 777. Section 1. All railroads shall furnish separate apartments in first-class coaches or separate first [class] coaches for the accommodation of white and colored passengers. Provided, equal accommodations are supplied to all persons, without distinction of race, color or previous condition, in such coaches.

Section 2. Any first-class coach may be divided into apartments, separated by a substantial partition, in lieu of separate coaches.

Section 3. Any railroad or agent violating the provisions of this act, is liable to a fine from $300 to $500 for each violation, to be collected by suit of any citizen.

Section 4. This act is not applicable to nurses on trains attending children or sick of the other race, nor to narrow guage roads, nor to relief trains in case of accident, nor to through vestibule trains, nor to officers or guards transporting prisoners, nor to prisoners being so transported.

Section 5. In case a coach for either white or colored passengers is full and another cannot be procured at the time, the conductor is authorized to set apart so much of the other coach as necessary.

Section 6. In addition to the first-class coaches provided for in this act, a second-class car shall be furnished in which it shall be lawful for any and all persons to ride by paying second-class fare or having a second-class ticket.

1900

Laws, 1900, p. 457. An act to amend the act of 1898, p. 777.

Section 1. The title is amended by striking out the words "or separate apartments in coaches" and so reading "An act to require all railroads and railroad companies operating trains and doing business in this state to provide and operate separate coaches for the accommodation and transportation of white and colored passengers in the state."

Section 2. Section 1 of the act is amended by striking out "Separate apartments in first-class coaches or separate first coaches" and so reading, "Shall furnish separate coaches for the accommodation, etc."

Section 3. Sections 2 and 6 of act repealed.

Act to read; Section 1 (as shown).

Section 2. The act is not to apply to nurses on trains attending children or sick of the other race, nor to narrow-guage roads, or branch lines, nor roads under forty miles in length, nor to relief trains in case of accident, nor to through vestibule trains not intended or used for local travel, nor to regular freight trains with a passenger coach attached for local travel, nor to officers nor guards transporting prisoners, nor to prisoners or lunatics being so transported.

Section 3. Railroads are not required to have second-class coaches or sell second-class tickets.

Section 4. It is unlawful for employees to permit white and colored people to occupy the same car, except as herein allowed. Violation of this act is a misdemeanor punishable by a fine from $25 to $100.

Section 5. Passengers remaining in another car than that provided for them are guilty of a misdemeanor and may be fined from $25 to $100. Conductors and employees are given the power to eject such passengers.

Laws, 1900, p. 443. An act establishing a state reformatory for criminals under the age of sixteen years. It provides: The white convicts shall be kept and employed separately from colored convicts. Part of the state farm in the County of Lexington is to be set apart for a reformatory exclusively for colored boys.

1903

Laws, 1903, p. 84. An act to amend the Separate Coach statute of Laws, 1900, p. 457. The act adds, "Provided, That all railroads operated by steam under forty miles in length shall furnish separate apartments for white and colored passengers; Provided further, that when said railroads under forty miles in length operate both a daily passenger train and a freight train, with or without a coach attached, said railroad shall be required to furnish separate apartments for white and colored passengers only on said passenger trains."

1904

Laws, 1904, p. 438. An act amending further Laws, 1900, p. 457. The act adds, "Steam ferries," and "cabins," and so reading, "All railroads and steam ferries engaged in this state as common carriers of passengers for hire, shall furnish separate coaches or cabins," etc.

1905

Laws, 1905, p. 954. Electric railways outside the corporate limits of cities and towns shall have authority to separate the races in their cars, and conductors are authorized and directed to separate the races in said cars.

Conductors and other employees of electric railways while in charge of cars are invested with the powers of peace officers and authorized to make arrests.

Conductors failing to separate the races may be fined not more than $100, or imprisoned for not more than thirty days for each offense.

1906

Laws, 1906, p. 133. An act establishing the South Carolina Industrial School. After this was established, the reformatory then in operation on the State Farm in Lexington County was directed to be used exclusively for colored boys.

Laws, 1906, p. 76. No persons, firms or corporations who or which furnish meals to passengers at station restaurants or station eating-houses, in times limited by common carriers of such passengers, shall furnish said meals to white and colored passengers in the same room, or at the same table, or at the same counter. Persons violating this act are guilty of a misdemeanor and may be fined from $25 to $100 or imprisoned not more than thirty days.

1910

Laws, 1910, p. 702. It is unlawful for a parent, guardian, etc., to give or surrender any white child permanently into the custody, control, maintenance or support of a negro. It is a misdemeanor, and the person may be fined or imprisoned in the discretion of the presiding judge. This does not apply to prevent the offices of a negro in the family of any white person as a nurse.

1911

Laws, 1911, p. 169. All able-bodied male convicts shall hereafter be sentenced to hard labor without regard to length of sentence. Provided that a separation of races shall be at all times observed, except in the penitentiary or on the state farms and in Kershaw County.

South Dakota

1867–1868

Laws of Dakota Territory, 1867–1868, p. 255. The word "white" was removed from the suffrage qualifications.

1909

Laws, 1909, Chapter 196, p. 297. Intermarriage, or illicit cohabitation, is forbidden between a person belonging to the African race, with any person belonging to the Caucasian race.

Violation of this act shall be a felony, punishable by a fine not exceeding $1,000, or by imprisonment not over ten years, or by both.

Any marriage in violation of the above shall be void from the beginning.

1913

Laws, 1913, Chapter 266, p. 405. Intermarriage, or illicit cohabitation, is forbidden between a person belonging to the Caucasian or White Race, and a person belonging to the African, Corean, Malayan, or Mongolian race.

Violation of this provision shall be a felony, punishable by a fine not exceeding $1,000, or by imprisonment in state prison not over ten years, or by both.

Section 2. No license shall be issued for any such marriage. Violation of this provision shall be a misdemeanor.

Section 3. Such a marriage shall be null and void from the beginning.

Tennessee

1865–1866

Laws, 1865–1866, Chapter 40. All free persons of color living together as husband and wife in this state, while in a state of slavery, are declared hereby to be man and wife, and the children are legitimate to as full extent as children of white citizens.

Laws, 1865–1866, Chapter 59. Administrators of free persons of color, deceased, leaving children that were slaves, are authorized to pay the estate to the children or heirs. Property of free persons of color or slaves shall be distributed agreeable to the laws of descent and distribution provided for free persons.

Laws, 1865–1866, p. 65. Separate schools are required for white and for negro children.

1868–1869

Laws, 1868–1869, Chapter 12. Section 13. No citizen of the state shall be excluded from the privileges of the University of Tennesee by reason of his race or color; but the accommodation and instruction of persons of color shall be separate from those for white persons.

1870

Constitution, 1870, Article IV. Section 1. Removes the limitation of the franchise to white persons.

Constitution, 1870, Article XI. Section 14. Intermarriage is prohibited between white persons and negroes, or descendants of negro ancestors to the third generation. The legislature shall enforce this by appropriate legislation.

Laws, 1870, Second Session, Chapter 39. Intermarriage of white persons with negroes, mulattoes or persons of mixed blood, descended from a negro to third generation, inclusive, or their living together as man and wife, is prohibited. Such marriage is null and void and a felony, punishable by imprisonment in the penitentiary from one to five years. The court may on recommendation of a jury, substitute fine and imprisonment in the county jail. (See Compiled Laws, 1821, Intermarriage prohibition; also Code, 1884, Sections 3291–3292, and Code, 1896, Sections 4186–4187.)

Laws, 1870, Second Session, Chapter 64. Section 40. The schools for white children and for colored children shall be kept separate and apart from each other, and the School Commissioners for each District shall strictly observe this requirement.

Constitution, Article XI. Section 12. Separate schools are required for white children and negro children. No school established or aided under this section shall allow both races to be received in the same school.

1873

Laws, 1873, p. 46. White and colored persons shall not be taught in the same school, but in separate schools under the same general regulations as to management, usefulness and efficiency.

1875

Laws, 1875, p. 216. The rule of common law giving a right of action to any person excluded from any hotel, or public means of transportation, or place of amusement, is hereby abrogated; and hereafter no keeper of any hotel or carrier of passengers for hire shall be bound or under any obligation to entertain, carry, or admit any person, whom he shall for any reason whatever choose not to entertain, carry or admit, nor shall any right exist in favor of any such person so refused, but the right of such keepers of hotels, carriers of passengers, and keepers of places of amusement to control the access or exclusion of persons shall be as perfect and complete as that of any private person over his private house. A right of action is given to any keeper of a hotel, common carrier and restaurant against any person guilty of turbulent conduct within or about the same; such person may be fined not less than

$100 and is liable to a forfeiture of $500; and the owner, or the person so offended, may sue in his own name for such forfeiture.

1881

Laws, 1881, Chapter 109. Section 3. The terms of admission for colored students given separate accommodations in schools shall be same as the terms prescribed for white students.

Laws, 1881, p. 139. Suitable but separate accommodations for colored students required, in the school for the blind at Nashville. An appropriation of $2,500 made for this purpose. The terms of admission for colored students must be the same as for white students.

Laws, 1881, p. 210. The State Board of Education was authorized to provide for the higher or the normal education of children of African descent.

Laws, 1881, p. 211. Whereas it is the practice of railroad companies to charge and collect from colored passengers first-class fare, and to compel said passengers to occupy second-class cars where smoking is allowed and no restrictions enforced to prevent vulgar or obscene language; therefore

All railroad companies shall furnish separate cars, or portions of cars cut off by partition walls, which all colored passengers who pay first-class rates of fare may have the privilege to enter and occupy.

The separate cars or apartments shall be kept in good repair, with the same conveniences, and subject to the same rules governing other first-class cars for preventing smoking and obscene language.

In case of failure to enforce the provisions of this law, the company shall pay a forfeit of $100, half to be paid to the person suing, the other half to be paid to the common school fund of the state.

Laws, 1881, First Extra Session, p. 7. Same as Laws, 1881, p. 210, with minor changes.

1882

Laws, 1882, Third Extra Session, p. 12. All persons paying first-class passenger rates are entitled to occupy first-class passenger cars. Railroads must furnish them such accommodations, under penalty of a fine of $300 payable to the common school fund. The laws of 1881, p. 211, are amended to be in conformity with this act.

1884

Code, 1844. Section 2367. If a company shall fail to enforce this law (as preceding), it shall pay $300, one-half to go to the person aggrieved, the other half to go to the common school fund, to be recovered at the suit of the person aggrieved, or of the superintendent of public instruction of the county where the offense is committed.

1885

Laws, 1885, p. 124. It is unlawful for owners, etc., of any places of public resort where a fee is charged for entrance to refuse admission to any person on account of the fact that such persons travel over a particular route, railway, etc., or in vehicles, carriages, etc., of any person or corporation rather than another. Nothing herein shall be construed as interfering with existing rights to provide separate accommodations and seats for colored and white persons at such places.

Laws, 1885, Extra Session, Chapter 19. Authorizing high-graded common schools. Nothing herein shall be construed so as to allow mixed schools of white and colored population, but such schools shall be taught separately as now provided.

1891

Laws, 1891, Chapter 52. Railroads other than street railroads shall provide equal but separate accommodations for the white and colored races by means of two or more passenger cars or by dividing passenger cars by a partition. It shall be permitted to take a nurse of another race in the car or compartment set aside for a different race. The act shall not apply to mixed and freight trains carrying only one passenger or combination passenger and baggage car. In such cases the one passenger car shall be partitioned into compartments. Conductors are required to assign passengers to their proper places.

Any railroad company refusing to comply with this act is guilty of a misdemeanor and may be fined from $100 to $500. Any conductor not carrying out the provisions of this act may be fined from $25 to $50.

1901

Laws, 1901, p. 9. It shall be unlawful for any school, college or place of learning to allow white and colored persons to attend the same school.

Section 2. It shall be unlawful for any teacher, professor or educator to allow the white and colored races to attend the same school, or for any teacher or other person to instruct or teach both the white and colored races in the same class, school, or college building, or in any other place or places of learning, or allow or permit the same to be done.

Section 3. Violation of this act or its provisions may be punished by a $50 fine, or imprisonment not less than thirty days or more than six months, or both.

Section 4. Grand juries shall have inquisitorial powers over all violations of this act.

1903

Laws, 1903, p. 75. Chapter 52 of Acts of 1891 is amended to include all street railroads in any county in the state having 150,000 inhabitants or over, as shown by the Federal census of 1900 or any subsequent Federal census. (Memphis was the only one in 1903.)

1905

Acts, 1905, p. 321. All street car lines must set apart or designate in each car a portion or certain seats for white passengers and also for colored passengers. Appropriate signs of designation must be posted. The conductor may change the designation when necessary in his judgment. An exception is made of nurses with children or with helpless persons of the other race. A refusal on the part of a street railroad company to provide separate parts of cars, as required, is punishable by a fine of $25 for each offense. Any passenger who refuses to take the proper seat is punishable by a fine of $25. Special cars may be run for one race exclusively.

Texas

1866

Constitution, 1866, Article VIII. Section 1. Africans and their descendants shall be protected in their rights of person and property by appropriate legislation. They shall have the right to contract and be contracted with; to sue and be sued, etc.

Constitution, 1866, Article VIII. Section 2. Africans shall not be prohibited on account of race or color from testifying as witnesses in any case, civil or criminal, involving injury to or crime against them in person or property.

Constitution, 1866, Article X. Section 7. All the taxes from Africans shall go to maintaining African schools; and it is the duty of the legislature to encourage colored schools. (Repealed by omission from the next Constitution, in 1876.)

Laws, 1866, p. 59. Negroes shall not testify except when the prosecution is against a negro, or when the alleged offense is against the person or property of a negro.

Laws, 1866, p. 97. Every railroad company shall attach to passenger trains one car for the special accommodation of freedmen. (Repealed in 1871.)

Laws, 1866, p. 131. All persons heretofore known as slaves or free persons of color, shall have the right to make and enforce contracts, sue and be sued, inherit, lease, hold, sell, and convey, etc.; and there shall be no discrimination in the criminal laws of the state. All prior contrary laws are repealed.

1869

Constitution, 1869, Article 12. Section 27. (Annotated Statutes, 1908, Sections 2616 and 2619.) All persons are legally married, who lived as husband and wife in slavery, and continued after emancipation to live together till the death of one, or till the adoption of this Constitution.

Constitution, 1869, Article III. Section 1. Removed the limitation of suffrage to white persons.

1870

Acts, 1870, p. 127. Slaves living as man and wife until the death of one party, shall be considered married and their issue legitimate.

1871

Laws, 1871, Second Session, p. 16. The equality of all persons before the law is recognized and shall ever remain inviolate, nor shall any citizen ever be deprived of any right, privilege or immunity, nor be exempted from any burdens or duty on account of race, color or previous condition of servitude.

Public carriers are prohibited from making any distinctions in the carrying of passengers. Such act is a misdemeanor punishable by a fine of from $100 to $500 or imprisonment from thirty to ninety days, or both. (Repeals Laws, 1866, p. 97.)

Laws, 1871, p. 108. There shall be no exclusion of any negro witness on account of color.

1876

Constitution, 1876, Article 7. Section 7. Separate schools with equal accommodation for white and colored children shall be provided.

Laws, 1876, p. 44. No school receiving white and colored pupils shall receive any of the public school fund.

Laws, 1876, p. 136. An Agricultural and Mechanical College for colored youths is established under supervision of the Board of Directors of Agricultural and Mechanical College in Brazos County.

Laws, 1876, Chapter CXX, p. 201. An act to establish the Public Free Schools. Section 15. A school fund is provided for the education alike of white and colored children. It shall be divided pro rata, according to the number of children of each race.

Section 19. All children from eight to fourteen years of age are entitled to the benefit of the free school fund without regard to race or color.

Section 53. A schoolhouse built in part by voluntary subscriptions by colored people for a colored school, shall not be used without their consent for white children; and the reverse.

Section 54. No school partly of white and partly of colored children shall receive aid from the school fund, but the two races shall always be taught in separate public free schools.

1879

Ex parte Francois, Federal Case No. 5047. Held that the difference of punishment in the law of 1858 against intermarriage was unconstitutional; but that the provision against intermarriage was constitutional. (See Laws, 1858, p. 164, prohibiting intermarriage and imposing different penalties on the white and black parties.)

Revised Statutes, 1879, Chapter I, Article 2843. Intermarriage law repeated. Penalty applied equally to both parties. (See Pen. C., 1915, X, I, Article 365.)

1884

Laws, 1884, p. 40. The same as the separate school provision of Laws of 1876, adding only a definition of the colored race and colored children, as being all persons of mixed blood, descended from negro ancestry to the third generation inclusive, although one ancestor of each generation may have been a white person.

1889

Laws, 1889, p. 132. Railroad companies shall maintain separate coaches for the white and the colored races. They shall be equal as to comfort. They shall be designated by words or letters, showing the race for whom intended. A compartment separated by a substantial partition with a door shall be sufficient. One part shall be exclusively for the colored race. Any passenger insisting on riding in an improper car or apartment is guilty of a misdemeanor, and shall be punished by fine not less than $5 or more than $20. Railroads shall have the right to regulate travel on all other coaches except the two coaches, or the double coach, set apart for the two races.

(The legislature suspended the rule requiring three consecutive days' reading of the bill, on account of approach of close of session.)

1891

Laws, 1891, p. 44. Separate coach law strengthened. Every railroad, lessee, manager or receiver thereof, doing business as common carriers for hire, shall provide separate coaches for white and negro passengers, which separate coaches shall be equal in all points of comfort and convenience. A substantial partition with a door shall be sufficient. They shall be designated by the name of the race posted in a conspicuous place in each compartment in plain letters. The law shall be posted in each coach and depot. Trains may carry chair cars or sleeping cars for the exclusive use of either race.

An exception to the provisions of the law is made for street railway cars. Also for nurses with employers, employees of a railroad in discharge of duties, freight trains carrying passengers in the caboose, and excursion trains run for the exclusive benefit of one race.

The conductor has authority to enforce the law. His wilful failure is a misdemeanor punishable by a fine from $5 to $25. The company refusing to provide separate accommodations may be fined from $100 to $1,000 for each trip. A passenger refusing to occupy the coash assigned may be fined from $5 to $25. (Three days' reading suspended, for emergency.)

Laws, 1891, p. 165. Same as preceding separate coach law, adding only the words "suburban railway cars," to the list of exceptions to the act.

1893

Laws, 1893, p. 198. (Three white trustees shall have charge of white schools.) Three colored trustees shall be elected or appointed, upon application of ten colored residents of any district, who shall manage the colored schools, under the direction of the white trustees of the district. (Separate school law repeated.)

1895

Laws, 1895, p. 29. School law of 1893, p. 198 amended. The three colored trustees become of full authority over colored schools, and are given sole charge. The three white and three colored trustees shall divide the school funds.

1897

Sayles Civil Statutes, 1897, Volume I, Article 2959. Intermarriage law. Persons of Caucasian blood or their descendants are forbidden to intermarry with persons of African blood or their descendants. Such marriage shall be void.

Sayles Civil Statutes, 1897, Article 4510. The term negro includes every person of African descent.

Sayles, 1897, Article 3885–3890. A normal school for colored teachers. One student not less than sixteen years old shall be admitted from the colored population of each senatorial district and three from the state at large. Students are bound to teach three years in the colored public schools of the state. They shall receive the same compensation as other teachers of public schools.

1905

Laws, 1905, p. 263. School Act, Section 96. The colored race and colored children are defined as "all persons of mixed blood, from negro ancestry." Section 130. Impartial provision for both races, and like education, shall be maintained.

1907

Laws, 1907, p. 58. Separate Coach Law. (Includes street-car companies.) Every railway company, street-car company and interurban railway company, lessee, manager, or receiver thereof, shall provide separate coaches or compartments for the accommodation of white and negro passengers, equal in all points of comfort and convenience. A good and substantial wooden partition with a door therein is sufficient, with words in plain letters indicating the race intended for. Each compartment of a street car or interurban car shall be divided by a board or marker placed in a conspicuous place, bearing appropriate words in plain letters indicating which race it is for.

Any railway company, street-car company or interurban company failing to provide separate coaches or compartments shall be fined from $100 to $1,000, each trip being a separate offense. A passenger wrongfully riding in an improper coach or compartment shall be guilty of misdemeanor, and fined from $5 to $25.

Exception is made of nurses with their employers, employees upon a train or cars in discharge of duty, freight trains carrying passengers in cabooses, and any excursion train, street car, or interurban car as such, for the benefit of either race. Companies may haul sleeping, dining, cafe, or chair-cars to be used exclusively by either white or negro passengers, separately but not jointly. This law shall be posted in a conspicuous place in each depot and coach.

Laws, 1907, p. 103. No white children can be adopted by a negro person, nor a negro child by a white person.

1909

Laws, 1909, Second Special Session, p. 401. Separate apartments shall be provided in all depot buildings for the use of white and of negro passengers.

1913

Laws, 1913, Special Session, p. 7. Texas Training School for boys under seventeen. White boys shall be kept, worked, and educated entirely separate from boys of other races, and kept apart in all respects.

1914

Vernon's Sayles Civil Statutes, 1914, Article 4553a. Sanitary Code for Texas. Rule 64. There shall be separate compartments and bedding, separate from white passengers, for negro porters in sleeping cars. Rule 65. Negro porters shall not sleep in sleeping car berths nor use bedding intended for white passengers.

1915

Penal Code, 1915, Title X, Chapter I, Article 346. Penalty for intermarriage is imprisonment in the penitentiary from two to five years.

Utah

1888

Laws, 1888, p. 88. Intermarriage is prohibited. (Original Law): Section 1, Marriage is prohibited and declared void, between a negro and a white person, and between a Mongolian and a white person.

1895

Constitution, 1895, Article III. Section 4. Public schools shall be open to all the children of the state.

1907

Laws, 1907, p. 32. Marriage laws amended. Intermarriage provision the same.

Vermont

1858

Laws, 1858, Chapter 37. Section 5. African descent shall not disqualify from citizenship of the state.

Virginia

1865

Laws, 1865–1866, p. 85. Where colored persons prior to February 27, 1866, agreed to occupy to each other the relation of husband and wife and were cohabiting as such at that date whether or not any ceremony had been performed, they shall be deemed husband and wife and their children legitimate, and when they ceased to cohabit before that date the children of the woman recognized by the man as his, shall be deemed legitimate. (1904 Code, p. 1,115, Section 2228.)

Laws, 1865–1866, p. 84. Every person having one-quarter or more of negro blood, shall be deemed a colored person, and every person not a colored person having one-quarter or more of Indian blood, shall be deemed an Indian.

Laws, 1865–1866, p. 89. Negroes and Indians may testify when a negro or an Indian is a party to the action.

1867

Laws, 1866–1867, p. 860. Negroes may testify as if they were white. (Repeals Laws, 1865–1866, p. 89.)

Constitution, 1867, Article III. Section 1. Male citizens are given the vote, removing limitation to white males.

1869–1870

Laws, 1869–1870, p. 413. White and colored persons shall not be taught in the same school, but in separate schools, under the same general regulations as to management, usefulness and efficiency. (See Laws, 1845–1846, p. 36.)

1870–1871

Laws, 1870–1871, p. 50. All male citizens from twenty-one to sixty who are entitled to vote and hold office, etc., shall be liable to serve as jurors, etc. (Reverses a law of 1852–1853, p. 43, excluding negroes.)

1871–1872

Laws, 1871–1872, p. 71. The state board of health shall keep a record of the causes of mortality among the colored population.

1872–1873

Laws, 1872–1873, p. 243. Gifts for purposes of the education of white persons, or likewise of colored persons, are valid.

1873

Code, 1873, p. 1,208. Any white person who shall intermarry with a negro shall be confined in jail not less than one year, and fined not less than $100. Performing such a ceremony is punishable by a fine of $200, of which one-half shall go to the informer (no penalty on negro). (See Code 1816, p. 401, and Code 1849, p. 471.)

1877–1878

Laws, 1877–1878, p. 28. Any person conspiring with another to incite the colored population of the state to make insurrection against the white population, or to incite the white population against the colored population, is liable to imprisonment in the penitentiary from five to ten years.

Laws, 1877–1878, p. 302. If any white person intermarry with a colored person, he shall be confined in the penitentiary not less than two or more than five years. If any person performs a marriage ceremony between white and colored persons he shall forfeit $200, of which the informer shall have half. Such marriages are absolutely void.

White and colored persons going out of the state to marry, shall be punished as if married in the state. (1910 Code, p. 1,119, Section 2253.)

1882

Laws, 1881–1882, p. 37. White and colored persons shall not be taught in the same school, but in separate schools under the same general regulations as to management, usefullness and efficiency. The determination as to who is a colored person lies with the board.

1896

Acts, 1895–1896, p. 352. Separation in schools, provision repeated. (See law of 1882.)

1900

Acts, 1899–1900, p. 301. Regulations for the government of a negro reformatory association to conduct reformatories for negro youth.

Acts, 1899–1900, p. 236. Railroads operating cars by steam on any railroad line, and all railroads doing business within this state, upon lines owned in part or in whole, or leased, and all foreign corporations who may be now, or may hereafter be, engaged in operating any of the railroads of this state, either in part or whole, either in their own name or that of others, are required to furnish separate cars for the transportation of white and colored passengers. Each compartment of a coach divided by a good and substantial partition with a door therein, shall be deemed a separate coach. In a conspicuous place, there shall be placed appropriate words in plain letters, indicating the race for which the compartment is intended. No difference or discrimination in quality, convenience or accommodation shall be made. Railroads neglecting to enforce this act are guilty of a misdemeanor, and may be fined from $300 to $1,000 for each offense.

Conductors, etc., are required to assign to each white or colored passenger his or her respective car, coach or compartment, "the conductors or managers acting in good faith, being for the purposes of this act the judge of the race of each passenger, and such passenger has refused to disclose his race." Any passenger may be put off a train if he refuses to occupy his assigned place. Conductors shall not be liable in damages therefor. A conductor failing to carry out the provisions of this act is guilty of a misdemeanor, with $25 to $50 fine for each offense. If the compartment or coach is completely filled and the increased number of passengers could not be foreseen, where no extra coaches or cars can be had, the conductor is authorized to set apart a portion assigned to passengers of one race to passengers of another race.

The act shall not apply to employees on railroads, or nurses, or an officer in charge of prisoners, or lunatics, white, colored, or both, or to prisoners or lunatics in his custody, or to transportation of passengers in a caboose car on freight trains, or to Pullman cars, or to through or express trains that do no local business. Circuit courts of counties and corporation courts of cities have jurisdiction of offenses under these sections.

Acts, 1899–1900, p. 340. 1294 f, Section 1. It shall be the duty of the captain and other officers of steamboats to assign white and colored passengers to their respective locations in separate sections. White and colored passengers shall be separate on all steamboats carrying passengers within the state, in the sitting, eating, and sleeping apartments as far as the construction of the boat and due consideration for the comfort of the passengers shall permit. There shall be no discrimination as to the quality of accommodations. The act shall not apply to nurses or attendants with their employers nor to officers in charge of prisoners or lunatics.

Section 2. Any officer of a steamboat failing to carry out these provisions shall be guilty of a misdemeanor, and subject to a fine of not less than $25 nor over $100.

Section 3. Any passenger refusing to occupy the accommodations set apart for his race shall be guilty of a misdemeanor, and fined not less than $5 nor more than $50, or confined in the jail not less than thirty days, or both. Such passenger may be ejected at any landing place. The company shall not be liable in damages therefor.

1901

Laws, 1901, Extra Session, p. 329. Same as 1899–1900, p. 340, leaving out the words, "as far as the construction of his boat and due consideration for the comfort of the passengers will permit."

Laws, 1901, Extra Session, p. 212. Separation is provided for on street railway cars between 29th and P Streets in the city of Richmond and Seven Pines in the County of Henrico.

1901–1902

Laws, 1901–1902, p. 639. Electric cars or trains within Alexandria, or from Alexandria to any point in the County of Alexandria, or from Alexandria to any point in the County of Fairfax, shall have separate coaches or compartments. No discrimination between accommodations for races is allowed. The conductor may increase or diminish the space allotted to either race.

Passengers failing to occupy the place set apart for their race are guilty of misdemeanor, and may be fined from $5 to $25. The conductor is authorized to eject such a passenger. No fare shall be returned in such a case. No damages shall be allowed therefor against the company. Conductors and employees are made special policemen for the enforcing of the law.

An exception to the provisions of law is made for employees of the company, nurses in attendance upon the other race, and officers in charge of prisoners.

1902

Constitutional Convention Registration Ordinance, for registration of voters prior to year 1904.

Section 4. Separate books of registration in duplicate, for white and colored voters, shall be kept in each precinct.

Constitution, 1902, Article 9. Section 140. Mixed schools are prohibited. White and colored children shall not be taught in the same school.

1904

Laws, 1904, p. 129. Any corporation operating sleeping, dining, palace, or compartment cars on the railroads in the state, is empowered to reject and to refuse admittance to any and all persons to enter into and ride in such sleeping, dining, palace, parlor, chair, or compartment cars, when in the discretion of such corporation, its conductors, agents or employees, it may be advisable to do so.

Code, 1904. Section 1313a. (The State Corporation Commission.)

Section 16. The commission may require the establishment by transportation companies of separate waiting-rooms at all stations, wharves, or landings for the white and the colored races.

Laws, 1904, p. 273. Owners of steamboat wharves shall provide separate and non-communicating rooms for the white and the colored races. This shall not apply to wharves at which boats arrive between 7 a. m. and 7 p. m. at which there are public houses open for the public and at which public comfort is cared for while waiting. Violation of the act is a misdemeanor punishable by a fine of from $5 to $20 for each offense.

1906

Laws, 1906, p. 12. Section 1. All companies operating trains or cars by electricity are authorized to separate white and colored passengers and to designate in each car a portion for white passengers and for colored passengers.

Section 2. No discrimination in quality shall be made. In cold weather they shall reasonably heat the several compartments.

Section 3. The conductor may increase or decrease the amount of space or seats set aside for either race, or may require any passenger to change his seat when and as often as he may deem necessary or proper.

Section 4. Failure to occupy the seats assigned is a misdemeanor and may be fined from $5 to $25. Such passenger may be ejected and is not entitled to the return of any part of the fare.

Section 5. Each conductor and motorman upon the cars shall be a special policeman for the enforcement of this act.

Section 6. Companies and employees are not liable in damages for any lawful act in enforcement of this law.

Section 7. Employees, nurses, and officers in charge of prisoners or lunatics are excepted from the provisions of the act.

Laws, 1906, p. 92. Amending 1906, p. 12. Previous Section 1, adds that neglecting to comply with the requirement is a misdemeanor, with $50 to $250 fine for each offense.

Section 3. Adds "Provided no contiguous seats or same bench shall be occupied by white and colored passengers at same time (unless and until all of the other seats in said car shall be occupied)." Also adds that any conductor failing to carry out the provisions of this section is guilty of a misdemeanor with $5 to $25 fine for each offense.

Section 5. Strengthens the rights of conductors and motormen as special policemen and conservators of the peace. "And, acting in good faith, he shall be, for the purpose of this act, the judge of the race of each passenger, whenever such passenger has failed to disclose his or her race."

1910

Laws, 1910, p. 581. Every person having one-sixteenth or more negro blood shall be deemed a colored person. Every person not a colored person having one-quarter or more Indian blood shall be deemed an Indian.

1912

Acts, 1912, p. 330–332, Chapter 157. Whereas, the preservation of the public morals, public health and public order, in the cities and towns of this commonwealth is endangered by the residence of white and colored people in close proximity to one another; therefore

1. Be it enacted by the general assembly of Virginia, That in the cities and towns of this commonwealth where this act shall be

adopted in accordance with the provisions of Section 11 hereof, the entire area within the respective corporate limits thereof shall, by ordinance, adopted by the council of each such city or town, be divided into districts, the boundaries whereof shall be plainly designated in such ordinance and which shall be known as "Segregation districts."

2. That no such district shall comprise less than the entire property fronting on any street or alley, and lying between any two adjacent streets or alleys, or between any street and an alley next adjacent thereto.

3. That the council of each such city or town shall provide for, and have prepared, within six months after such council shall have adopted the provisions of this act, a map showing the boundaries of all such segregation districts, and showing the number of white persons and colored persons residing within such segregation district, on a date to be designated in such ordinance of adoption, but which shall be within sixty days of the passage of such ordinance; and such map shall designate as a white district each district wherein there are, on the date so designated, more residents of the white race than there are residents of the colored race, and shall designate as a colored district each district so defined, in which there are on the said date as many or more residents of the colored race, as there are residents of the white race.

4. That after twelve months from the passage of the ordinances adopting the provisions of this act, it shall be unlawful for any colored person, not then residing in a district so defined and designated as a white district, or who is not a member of a family then therein residing, to move into and occupy as a residence any building or portion thereof in such white district, and it shall be unlawful, after the expiration of said period of twelve months from the passage of the ordinance adopting the provisions of this act, for any white person not then residing in a district so defined and designated as a colored district, or who is not a member of a family then therein residing, to move into and occupy as a residence any building, or portion thereof, in such colored district.

5. That any person occupying any room as a sleeping place in any district, whether as a dependent, boarder or lodger, shall be classed as a resident of such district, unless it appear that such

occupation was merely transitory and that such person had another fixed place of abode.

6. That the said map shall be certified by the clerk of the council of such city or town, and shall be at all times kept open to inspection by the public in the office of such clerk, and that any person considering that such map has not been prepared in accordance with the provisions of this act, and who is in any wise prejudiced thereby, shall, within sixty days of the completion thereof, or within eight months from the adoption of the provisions of this act by such city or town, notify the clerk of said council in writing of the particulars of the error claimed to have occurred in the preparation of such map, and such person may thereafter within thirty days after giving such notice move the corporation court of such city, or if there be no such court, the circuit court of the county wherein such city or town is situate, or the judge of such court in vacation, to correct the error complained of, and the said court or the judge thereof in vacation, shall investigate the facts in the premises, and order such corrections of such map as may be necessary to make the same conform to the provisions of this act.

7. That the map so prepared and certified and corrected, shall be prima facie evidence of the boundaries and racial designation of such districts.

8. That any person who, after the expiration of twelve months from the passage of the ordinance of adoption, shall reside in any such district, contrary to the provisions of this act, shall be guilty of a misdemeanor, and upon conviction thereof, shall be fined for the first week of such prohibited residence not less than $5 nor more than $50, and for each succeeding day of such residence the sum of $2.

9. That nothing herein contained shall preclude persons of either race employed as servants by persons of the other race from residing upon the premises of which such employer is the owner or occupier.

10. That nothing herein contained shall be construed or operate to prevent any person who on the date on which this act shall be adopted in any city or town, shall have acquired a legal right to occupy as a resident any building, or portion thereof in any such district, in such city or town, whether by devise, purchase, lease

or other contract, and who shall not, on the date which this act shall be so adopted have actually moved into such premises, from thereafter moving into and occupying the same.

11. That this act shall apply only to the cities or towns which by a recorded vote of a majority of the members elected to the council thereof, or if there be two branches of such council by a recorded vote of a majority of the members elected to each branch thereof, shall adopt the provisions of this act and in all respects comply with the requirements hereof.

1916

Acts, 1916, p. 60. Amending Acts 1912, p. 330, by adding "provided that nothing herein shall be construed to take away from any city or town not adopting this act, any power or authority it may have to pass ordinances regulating the segregating of the residences of white and colored persons, and all such ordinances heretofore passed by cities and towns not adopting this act are hereby ratified and confirmed, to the same extent as if the said cities and towns had been specially thereunto authorized.

Acts, 1916, p. 41. An act as to negro minors committed to the Negro Reformatory Association, and providing for the same compensation to be paid by the state to the association as jailers were entitled to, up to the number of 200 negro minors.

Washington

1854–1855

Laws, 1854–1855, p. 33. Section 1. All marriages heretofore solemnized in this territory where one of the parties shall be a white person and the other possessed of one-quarter or more negro blood, or more than one-half Indian blood shall be void.

Section 2. Any judge or clergyman solemnizing such marriage may be fined from $50 to $500, the money to be for the use of the common schools.

Section 3. Nothing shall be construed to prevent parties from being united in marriage who may be living together at the time of passage of this act.

1865–1866

Laws, 1865–1866, p. 81. Section 2, Clause 3. Where either of the parties is a white person and the other a negro or Indian, or a person of half or more negro or Indian blood, any marriage shall be prohibited. (Approved January 20, 1866.)

1866

Laws, 1866, p. 91. No one shall be incompetent as a witness by reason of having negro blood.

1867–1868

Laws, 1867–1868, p. 47. Be it enacted, That the third clause of Section 2 of an act entitled "An act to regulate marriages, approved January 20, 1866," be stricken out.

1889–1890

Laws, 1889–1890, p. 524. Civil Rights Act. It includes the enjoyment of "inns, public conveyances on land or water, theaters, and other places of public amusement, and restaurants, subject only to conditions and limitations established by law and applicable alike to all citizens of whatever race, color, or nationality."

Section 2. Violation of the law is a misdemeanor punishable by from $50 to $300 fine, or from thirty days to six months' imprisonment.

1895

Laws, 1895, p. 192. Civil Rights Act is amended to read as follows: "Inns, restaurants, eating-houses, barber shops, public conveyances on land and water, theaters, and other places of public accommodation and amusement."

1909

Laws, 1909, p. 1027. Section 434. (Civil Rights Law further enacted). Every person who shall deny, because of race, creed, or color, the full enjoyment of any of the accommodations or privileges of any place of public resort, accommodation, assemblage, or amusement, shall be guilty of a misdemeanor.

1910

Code, 1910. Section 2304. Repeal. "Note: In view of the general nature of the title of this act (1909, p. 890) a doubt exists as to the schedule of acts repealed. Accordingly, in so far as the repealed acts seem not in conflict with other provisions of this act, or not clearly embraced in the title of this act, they are all retained." (In the 1910 Code.) (This includes, among many other sections, Section 2726 to 2762 inclusive, covering Civil Rights, Section 2761–2762).

R. and B.'s Code, 1910. Section 2760. All persons within the State of Washington are entitled to the full and equal enjoyment of the public accommodations and privileges of inns, restaurants, eating-houses, barber shops, public conveyances on land or water, theaters, or other places of public accommodation and amusement, subject only to conditions and limitations established by law and applicable alike to all citizens.

Section 2761. Violation of this act or aiding or inciting such denial is a misdemeanor, punishable by a fine from $50 to $300, or by imprisonment from thirty days to six months.

1912

Pierce's Code has only the Civil Rights Act of 1909, p. 1027, Section 434 as Tit. 135, Section 867 of Code.

West Virginia

1860

Laws, 1860, p. 529. All marriages between a white person and a negro are void. (Code, Va., 1860.)

1863

Constitution, 1861–1863, Article III. Section 1. The franchise is limited to whites.

1865

Laws, 1865, p. 50. There shall be separate schools for negroes, where there are more than thirty negro children in a school district. If the average daily attendance is less than fifteen for a month, the school is to be discontinued for any period not exceeding six months. If there are less than thirty children in the school district, or the attendance is less than fifteen, the money is to be used for negro education as the board thinks best.

1866

Laws, 1866, p. 102. All marriages heretofore celebrated between colored persons, if in good faith, and both were living together as husband and wife on February 28, 1866, shall be deemed valid. All persons who were cohabiting together, whether rites had been performed or not, shall be deemed husband and wife, and all their children shall be deemed legitimate. When they have ceased to cohabit, all the children of the woman, recognized by the man to be his, shall be deemed to be legitimate.

Laws, 1866, p. 85. No person shall be incompetent as a witness on account of race or color.

1867

Laws, 1867, p. 44. Slightly modifies the Constitution of Virginia as to juries. Limits them to white male persons.

1870

Code, 1870, p. 579. Section 1. All white male persons from twenty-one to sixty years of age, are liable to service as jurors.

1872

Constitution, 1872, Article XII, Section 8. White and colored persons shall not be taught in the same school.

Laws, 1872–1873, Chapter 47. Section 3. Only white persons shall serve as jurors.

Laws, 1872–1873, Chapter 161. All laws in force in this State regulating marriages, or registration of births, deaths, and marriages, shall apply to colored persons the same as to white persons, but such records shall be kept in separate books.

Laws, 1872–1873, p. 502. Repeats law of 1866, p. 102, as to colored marriages.

Laws, 1872–1873, p. 391, Chapter 123. Section 17. White and colored persons shall not be taught in the same school. There shall be a free colored school where there are twenty-five or more colored children.

Section 18. When in a district the benefit of a free school is not secured to colored children, the fund applicable to the support of free schools in such district shall be divided in the proportion which the number of colored children bear to the number of white children and the share of the former shall be set apart for the education of the colored children in each district and be applied for that purpose from time to time.

1881

Laws, 1880, Chapter 15. An act providing for normal training for colored teachers.

Acts, 1881, p. 176. Separate school law repeated. The required number must exceed fifteen negro children for a colored school.

1882

Acts, 1882, Chapter 123, p. 349. Intermarriage. Any white person who shall marry a colored person shall be confined in jail not more than one year, and fined not exceeding $100.

Any person who shall knowingly perform the marriage ceremony between a white person and a negro shall be guilty of a misdemeanor and be fined not exceeding $200. (Code, 1913, Sec. 5311, 5312.)

Acts, 1882, p. 186. All male persons shall be liable to service as jurors.

1889

Laws, 1889–1890, p. 87. If colored troops are organized, they shall be enlisted and kept separate from other troops, in separate companies and regiments.

Laws, 1889, p. 15. White and negro inmates of the reform school for boys shall be kept separate.

1897

Acts, 1897, Chapter 8. White and colored girls shall be kept separate in the industrial home.

Acts, 1897, p. 42. Insane asylums shall have separate wards for negro and for white patients.

1901

Laws, 1901, p. 159. Separate school law repeated. The required number of negro children must exceed ten for a colored school.

Wisconsin

1848

Constitution 1848, Article III, Section 1. Voting is limited to white citizens.

1849

Laws, 1849, p. 85. An act providing for the submission to popular vote of the question of negro suffrage in the State. It provided for a separate ballot at the general election to vote on the question of negro suffrage. If this should carry, Section 2 should be a law.

Section 2. Any negro residing one year in the State shall be eligible to hold any office.

In November, 1849, the election on African suffrage was held. For suffrage, 5,265 votes were cast, and against it, 4,075. This was not a majority equal to a majority of all the votes cast at such election for the offices voted for at the same time. The Board of Canvassers in 1849 declared that a majority of votes had not been cast for suffrage.

1865

Laws, 1865, p. 517. A proposed amendment to the Constitution, extending negro suffrage, was passed by the legislature, but rejected when submitted to popular vote.

1866

Gillespie v. Palmer, 20 Wisconsin, 544 (1866). The Supreme Court held that the right to vote had been granted to the negro by the Act of 1849 and the subsequent vote of the people at the general election of November 6, 1849. The Court held unanimously that the law meant a majority of votes cast upon the subject, and that the action of the legislature and the people since that time had taken place without serious thought and consideration.

1895

Laws, 1895, p. 428, Chapter 223. (*Statutes, 1915. Section 4398.*) Any person who shall deny in whole or in part the accommodations of any inns, restaurants, saloons, barber shops, eating houses, public conveyances on land or water, or any other place of public accommodation or amusement, except for reasons applicable alike to all persons of every race or color, or who shall aid or incite such denial, or require any person to pay a larger sum than the regular rate charged other persons for such accommodations or privileges, is liable to pay to the person aggrieved not less than $5 with costs, and shall also be punished by a fine of not more than $100, or confinement in the county jail not exceeding six months, or both; judgment for one to bar the other.

Wyoming

1887

Revised Statutes, 1887. Section 3947. When there are fifteen or more colored children within any school district, the board of directors thereof, with the approval of the county superintendent of schools, may provide separate schools for the instruction of such colored children.

1889

Constitution, 1889, Article I. Section 3. The laws of this State affecting the political rights and privileges of its citizens shall be without distinction of race, color, sex, or any circumstance or condition whatsoever other than individual incompetency, or unworthiness duly ascertained by a court or competent jurisdiction.

Vita

The author of this study was born September 1, 1875. He received the degree of A.B. from the University of Chicago, in 1896. During the years 1896–1898 and 1913–1914 he was a graduate student in Columbia University. He graduated from the Rochester Theological Seminary in 1903 and was ordained to the ministry. In 1914 he became head of the Department of Social Service of the University of Toronto. As a student in Columbia University he studied under Professors Giddings, Seligman, Chaddock, John Bassett Moore, F. J. Goodnow, Devine, and Lindsay. He received the degrees of LL.B. and A.M. from Columbia in 1898.

www.ingramcontent.com/pod-product-compliance
Lightning Source LLC
LaVergne TN
LVHW091635100826
845152LV00002B/43

9781584777519